Increasing Competence through Collaborative Problem-Solving

Using Insight into Social and Emotional
Factors in Children's Learning

Gerda Hanko

David Fulton Publishers

London

David Fulton Publishers Ltd
Ormond House, 26–27 Boswell Street, London WClN 3JD

First published in Great Britain by David Fulton Publishers 1999

Note: The right of Gerda Hanko to be identified as the author of this work has been asserted by her in accordance with the Copyright, Designs and Patents Act 1988.

Copyright © Gerda Hanko 1999

British Library Cataloguing in Publication Data

A catalogue record for this book is available from the British Library

ISBN 1-85346-600-X

Typeset by FSH, London
Printed in Great Britain by The Cromwell Press, Trowbridge, Wilts.

Contents

For simplicity alone (with no sexist implications) staff and children alike are referred to by the masculine pronoun

Acknowledgements

In the course of the work described in this book I have enjoyed meeting and being stimulated by a great number of people, all of whom I want to thank.

First of all I am indebted to the late Irene Caspari for introducing me to the possibilities of consultation as a mode of working with teachers and student teachers in the classroom context, when she began, three decades ago, to demonstrate the approach at University Education Departments, and to Elizabeth Irvine and Elsie Osborne, both leading practitioners in the field of interprofessional consultation, for their continuing interest and encouragement, until their recent deaths, to develop this collaborative model further.

I also want to express my thanks to the staffs of the teacher education departments, professional development centres, psychological and education support services and professional organisations who invited me to work with them, for the invaluable exchange of ideas and experience that this entailed; above all to the teachers and head teachers of schools whose active and evaluative participation in the groups constantly offered me fresh indications of the kind of support that they could use and helped me to attempt to develop practice and principles for charting this area of work within a continuing professional development structure.

My very special thanks are due to Ken Millins, Chris Thompson and Liz Udloff who not only read the typescript but commented on it most helpfully while sharing their valuable professional expertise with me.

Preface

This book is about the use of a specific collaborative problem-solving approach as part of a Continuing Professional Development policy. The national drive towards achieving academic excellence for all currently dominates educational debate and practice. The Teacher Training Agency (1998) states, as one of its principal aims, the promotion of effective and efficient professional development (since this) will have the maximum impact on pupils' learning. The Department for Education and Employment in its White Paper *Excellence in Schools* emphasises the importance of valuing and supporting teachers as 'going hand-in-hand [with] ensuring that the best methods available are used in every classroom in the country' (DfEE 1997a). Articles on Collaborative Models of Developing Competence have tried to 'identify those elements in managing the process of CPD that have made these initiatives effective' (Smith 1996). Creese, Norwich and Daniels surveyed the perceived usefulness of collaborative teacher groups in the special needs area, and, finding these groups 'clearly important at many different levels, most obviously in sustaining and increasing teacher morale and confidence, and thereby contributing to a positive ethos in the school' (Creese *et al.* 1998, pp. 109–114), suggest their wider use as desirable. Likewise, while earlier editions of my own book on Staff Support focused on the special emotional, behavioural and learning needs of some children, feedback from teachers led me to conclude the third edition (Hanko 1995) by recommending a collaborative problem-solving approach to staff development as a sound basis for implementing full curricular entitlement for all.

The DfEE emphasis on valuing and supporting teachers suggests an awareness of the difficulties involved in the task of raising all children's academic achievements when teachers themselves are suffering from previous unwittingly dysfunctional educational legislation. An excessively 'results'-centred teaching climate had devalued teachers' professionalism and severely reduced their opportunities to attend to that 'living link'*, the emotional and social factors which profoundly affect all children's learning. As Warnock (1996) fears, such a climate cannot but lead to academic failure for some. Others remind teachers of the part played by the emotions as offering 'a stimulation and enhancement of pupils' learning, [but] in negative form can be a killer of it' (Wragg 1997).

With growing recognition that 'the emotional development of children must continue to be a central concern for mainstream education' (DfE 1994), many teachers are now concerned that there is in current official documents little reference to its importance or to an 'affective curriculum' as the Elton Report (DES 1989) had advocated. Consequently, teachers have come to perceive the official view on quality in teaching and on achieving excellence as still an almost exclusively academic matter. In the light of complex social and educational problems, 'supporting teachers to ensure that the best methods are available for the achievement of all children's academic potential' (DfEE 1997a) will therefore require an approach to staff development that addresses the importance of the relationship between social/emotional development and academic progress at all stages of school attendance.

Collaborative staff development programmes – now envisaged in a DfEE (1998) Programme of Action – can assist teachers in responding more appropriately, as an integral part of their daily professional task, to the learning needs of pupils with emotional and behavioural problems. Teachers thereby found that almost imperceptibly their own professional development was promoted because it also enhanced their overall competence with all their pupils. This in turn assisted them in meeting current as well as evolving needs.

It therefore seems appropriate to extend the material I have been able to offer to date, to take it beyond the special needs context, and to focus on the extent to which a well structured school-based or school-focused collaborative support network can help teachers to attend to the affective/social dimension of an academic curriculum, to aid all pupils learning. (Some parts of the text are derived from the third edition of my book on Staff Development (Hanko 1995)).

> *To docket living things past any doubt
> You cancel first the living spirit out.
> The parts lie in the hollow of your hand,
> You only lack the living link you banned.

> Goethe, *Faust* (transl. Philip Wayne Penguin, 1949)

> Gerda Hanko
> London
> November 1998

Introduction

Teachers are deeply concerned with their pupils as people but may be unaware of some of their pupils' hidden needs which they may not recognise. A majority of children may lead a relatively uncomplicated life which allows them to enjoy what their teachers can offer them. Many others do not. Where teachers are aware of problems, however, they may be convinced that there is little they can do about it ('we are not trained that way') or feel that this is not part of their remit ('we are not social workers or psychologists').

They may be baffled by talented teenagers who are failing to develop their talents, or be unaware of those gifted children who already in Year 1 'take careful deceptive measures to hide their giftedness, like conforming to the class norm by pretending they can't read, pretending not to know the answers to questions, holding back from classroom discussion' (Freeman 1996, see also Eyre 1997). Teachers may worry, feel frustrated or despondent about the quiet child who refuses to respond to their efforts of inviting participation (Collins 1996), or those who are 'absent without leaving, playing truant in mind' (Collins 1998a). There are the undiscovered targets of bullying of which not even their parents are aware (nobody knew of Vijay's ordeal until after his suicide, the teenager who never missed a day at school, wrote an excellent essay on bullying for which his teacher gave him a merit mark without realising what his essay was really about (Boseley 1997).

There are those who at playtime suffer deeply from being ostracised or from being just less popular, who go through crises in peer relationships which carry over into lesson time, while others are burdened with feelings and responsibilities that arise from living with a severely impaired member of the family or a chronically sick sibling (which may lead to early competence or childhood deprivation). According to a 1997 survey (Anthony Clare, BBC Radio 4, 7.10.1998) 23% of all children, and 20% of primary school children experience this situation. Over 125,000 children have a parent in prison (see Tony's case, pp.19–24) but shame often forces them to hide the fact (Williams 1998) (also Redwood 1998). There are those worried about family break up and about their parents' preoccupation with their own difficulties 'leading to less expressive parent–child relationships (and/or) rebellion towards changing family situations' (Pagani *et al.* 1998).

There are those who still grieve over past bereavement ('he will have got over it by now'), or are worried about family break up. There are the multiple-school attenders ranging from Forces children from otherwise stable families to 'looked after' children in care and children from traumatised refugee families. There are the isolated childhoods where we don't ask (W. H. Auden's *Unknown Citizen* 'Are they free, are they happy? The question is absurd. Had anything been wrong, we should certainly have heard') until we hear of the lonely childhoods of the murderous Dunblane and Hungerford perpetrators. There are the disaffected 'middle achievers' whose poor basic skills impede their enjoyment. And there are those whose 'aggressive or withdrawn facade may mask constant misery, loneliness, self-loathing and fear (Yapp 1991, see also Graham and Hughes 1995). Symptoms of depression, when externalised, tend 'not to be seen' as such by teachers or parents (Graham and Hughes 1995, Puura *et al.* 1998), and, where externalised as oppositional behaviour, may 'mask their cognitive competence' to the children themselves and to their teachers (cf. Fagot and Leve 1998). Without an understanding of the emotional aspect of defiance, teachers may dismiss the defiance of insecurely attached children as 'mere attention-seeking' rather than seeing in it a possible longing for gaining control over at least something in their lives (Barkley 1997) – a wish for control which sensitive teaching could well deflect into the learning task (Hanko 1994).

The specific joint problem-solving approach presented here, is about the rich diversity of professional expertise which can be enhanced in every school, and about the wide range of needs to be met in every classroom. It is about the sharing process that, by maximising existing expertise, can help teachers to respond more appropriately to those needs in order to achieve that 'excellence for all' which schools are expected to aim for.

The approach has been developed in response to the multiplying demands from teachers to receive the kind of support that will help them to meet pupils' emotional and social needs within a normal teaching day, through curriculum content and delivery, teacher–pupil and classroom relationships and the involvement of parents as partners. This approach has been welcomed by schools in many parts of the country (as well as in other parts of Europe) as a model for the development of in-service support systems, eliciting teachers' hidden skills to motivate 'difficult' children with re-educative challenges, demonstrating how a sensitive curricular response can not only help to meet the emotional and social learning needs of specific children, but can enhance the quality of teaching and learning in the classroom as a whole (Mongon and Hart 1989). Who said it first that so-called 'problem children' are like other children, only more so?

It is hardly surprising that teachers who have been helped to deepen their understanding and to respond more appropriately to the behavioural, emotional and learning needs of those pupils who confronted them with particular difficulties have also found that emotional and social factors affect not only failure to learn but play a part in all learning. Promoting such insight, and enabling teachers to apply such insight in the daily process of teaching and learning, would therefore appear to be at a premium, whatever their pupils' achievement.

How does continuing *collaborative* problem-solving assist *individual* teachers in enhancing their competence for meeting the diverse learning needs of their pupils? The relevant issues relate to professional development and militating obstacles such as the difficulties that teachers experience in identifying their own needs and in optimising existing provision. Providers may experience difficulty in gearing their provision to the context in which teachers work, to be of both *immediate* and *long-term* use in the classroom and school setting. How to offer this in such a way that it is usable and acceptable while maintaining teachers' professional autonomy, and to ascertain who might be in a position – whether within the school or external to it – of initiating staff development groups and possess the professional skills required from effective supporters is an additional challenge.

Genuinely collaborative provision rules out prescriptive advice and intrusive exhortations on what a school or a teacher should do, as fundamentally ineffective. Instead, it recognises, appreciates and builds on teachers' existing strengths and expertise. Ultimately, it creates conditions favourable to finding workable solutions and produces a climate of commitment and mutual respect in which the teachers themselves, as individuals and as a genuinely collaborative team, implement their conclusions and observe and consider what needs evolve.

Teachers welcome such viable support. To ensure such viability, for the benefit of all children regardless of attainment, a range of questions needs to be asked. How aware are we as teachers of the factors that influence children's learning; of the perception which children, their parents and teachers themselves have of each other; and of the effect that these can have on work in the classroom? How much insight into emotional and social factors in learning and their link with learning needs can be of help to teachers in mainstream schools and therefore ought to be made available to them? How can they, often so overworked and under stress, best acquire such insight and information so that they are of immediate and long-term use to them and to the children? What skills do those who offer support to teachers need themselves, to be able to extend those of their teaching colleagues?

Norwich invites us to consider children's educational needs as falling into three groups: those needs which are common to all, those which are common to some, and those which are unique to each individual (Norwich 1996b, 1998; O'Brien 1998a, b). An education system charging its teachers with helping all children without fear or favour to learn to the best of their potential, will have to accommodate all three. Accepting 'emotional development as a central concern for mainstream education' (DfE 1994), and acknowledging that emotional and social factors play a part in every child's learning, requires teachers, as an integral part of their task, to examine how best they can hold in balance commonality and difference with regard to emotional and social needs.

Such hidden needs as listed above hinder children's learning and, if they remain unmet, worsen as they further impede progress. There are also general behaviour problems, not themselves expressive of deep-seated needs, which teachers need to deal with to benefit the personal development and educational progress of all. Teachers may, however, be baffled by children who seem to obstruct their best efforts to help, and be made to feel useless, not understanding what underlying needs the behaviour expresses. They may find some behaviour provoking reactions in them which increase rather than reduce the problem. They may fall back on defensive encounters with disaffected pupils who may then continue, in what may seem to them an ongoing war, to indicate their needs in 'unmanageable' ways which educational institutions, and indeed, society, must find unacceptable. This may lead to exclusion.

Teachers may blame the children and their background for their difficulties, see the problem as located in the child, in his family and home or in the child's situation at school, in conflict with what is expected of him. They may feel that official demands and pressures in the system are interfering with their ability to respond adequately to such children's needs and indeed 'may lead to academic failure for some' (Warnock 1996). Either way, they may feel that they have to handle the difficulties predominantly in terms of control, feel compelled to resort to merely coping, which they may themselves despise but which allows them to keep going at a reduced level of functioning and a growing level of stress. As the Elton Report (DES 1989) had shown, many teachers battle on without the professional and emotional support which they could receive from those trained to offer it. Many children whom teachers could in fact help within their *educational* remit and the constraints of the system, tend not to receive the help to which they would in all probability have been able to respond. Thus, teachers could be spared much distress, and much waste of emotional and educational potential could be prevented, if some of the principles, pedagogical procedures and practical support skills would be made generally available to them.

These will be the twin issues to be addressed in the chapters that follow. Part I studies offer insight into the social and emotional aspects of children's learning, and show that their importance must be recognised and be harnessed to professional competence. Then the principles are discussed of a collaboratively consultative problem-solving approach, geared to such competence. The framework of that approach is described in relation to the different theoretical bases and practices employed and their relevance to school practicalities. Examples of case discussions in a range of school-based settings will show how teachers, through skilled sharing of their experience, learned to contribute to their colleagues' and their own expertise and became more aware of how communication processes become most effective.

Part II shows how the daily curriculum, ordinary classroom and school procedures are used to address children's emotional and social realities as a source of learning experiences relevant to the needs of all pupils. This is followed by a section on effective collaboration with parents and by one on cooperation between institutions and services.

Part III offers guidelines for initiating and developing collaborative training groups in a variety of settings and summarises the possibilities of a joint problem-solving approach for meeting the needs of both teachers and pupils. It addresses the question of 'Who supports the supporters?' and deals with the training and support needs of those in a position to develop this work, such as staff development tutors from training institutions and schools, a school's in-service, special needs, pastoral care or curriculum coordinators, other colleagues accepted as having advanced skills in supporting their fellow professionals, mentors charged with the induction of new teachers, members of the psychological and education support services, specialist schools staff engaged in outreach work, or independent providers. All of these may be able or could be enabled to share their skills and understanding in a way that can be applied by teachers as an integral part of their professional task of attending to the range of needs in their classrooms.

PART I

Enriching the Learning Environment for Pupils and Teachers: Maximising Existing Expertise

Chapter 1

Social and Emotional Factors as Aspects of Cognition

This chapter focuses on understanding how children's emotional and social experiences may affect their learning and on the extent to which teachers should use such understanding in aid of it in the classroom. The word 'emotional' is a difficult word in the English language. When used in an educational context it can give rise to ambivalent interpretations and unwarranted attacks as an 'elevation of feeling over reason'. Nor are terms like 'emotional education' or an 'emotional curriculum' very helpful to those who agree with the DfE's emphasis on the importance of children's emotional development as a central concern for mainstream education (DfE 1994). To forestall such polarisations, a quick reminder of available complementary workable paradigms about the interactive nature of emotional, social and cognitive development may be useful. They permit us to recognise the limits of any one ideology and to work with multiple concepts (Norwich 1996a).

Piaget's and Kohlberg's theory of stages of cognitive development and moral learning gives a developmental account of reasoning, of how rules are conceived and followed and how children learn to see things from somebody else's point of view. Psychodynamic schools of psychology analyse rational and irrational emotional expression and how feelings may originate and develop from social experiences. Applied to curriculum studies this would suggest that we learn best when we care most and that emotional involvement plays an important part in learning. Kubie speaks of the right to know what one feels and that children need to be helped to *understand* their loves and hates, their fears and curiosities, their strained and stressful relationships. Social learning schools suggest coordinating emotional, social and cognitive growth through normal daily classroom encounters, utilising children's spontaneous happenings as well as those introduced and created by the teacher. Bruner, in his seminal course on 'Man', emphasises the knowledge-getting process with reference to the nature of the child as learner who 'learns to master himself, disciplines his taste, deepens his view of the world' (Bruner 1968) as his emotional energies are engaged. Erikson's life cycle theory, attributing specific tasks for each phase of development (such as the development of basic trust in childhood), suggests a wide scope for teachers.

An education of the emotions or educating children in social competence, by definition, has a cognitive dimension. Misunderstandings abound where these are seen as additional to an academic curriculum. Thus mere references to social aspects frequently lead to pseudo-social grouping practices where no real social learning takes place. Insight into social and emotional factors as aspects of children's learning, and using such insight effectively, thus makes the issue one of professional competence.

Social factors in learning

Bennett (1991) exposes the 'aridity of mere classroom grouping practices' with children merely sitting together but being engaged solely in individual work, and contrasts these with the true impact of social processes on children's performance through genuinely cooperative approaches. He describes how cooperative group endeavours provided children with social and emotional experiences, such as giving and receiving explanations, which did indeed improve learning, and that the sharing of knowledge between children and between children and teacher facilitated task enhancing talk. Teachers who were offered training in cooperative group work were impressed by how much the children enjoyed it, and reported how surprised they were that 'the children were in fact able to use each other and help each other more than [I] realised'. They were delighted how for instance a cooperative poetry activity developed the conditions for high quality learning to take place. The results were greater enjoyment, independence, cooperation and better quality work from both low and high attainers.

The current national emphasis on standards in literacy will require an equally strong emphasis on the effectiveness of cooperative teaching methods for raising standards. This underlines the need for teachers to find their own best ways of improving on merely prescribed statutory requirements. Enhancing teachers' competence through using their insight into the affective/social dimensions in both learning and teaching would be a case in point.

Bennett refers to Vygotsky's concept of the 'zone of proximal development' as that stage at which 'learning awakens a variety of internal developmental processes that are able to *operate only when the child is interacting with people in his environment and in cooperation with (his) peers*' (italics added). Bennett asks 'Can we design tasks (for instance) in maths, science and technology that generate abstract talk? Can children be trained to function more effectively in groups, at both a social and intellectual level? What should the nature of teacher intervention be in cooperative group work?' (Bennett 1991).

Vygotsky's work on the links between learning and small group social interaction, social dialogue, language and knowledge has led a number of British educators to study its educational implications. Daniels (1993) discusses the individual in the organisation and comments on the importance of understanding the relation between the social conditions of learning and development and of speech serving to mediate social processes. Pollard (1993), studying innovative practices in primary schools, emphasises how group work shows the capacity of children to construct their understanding *together*, in subjects like mathematics, science, design technology, and in 'process writing' in English which encourages children to draft, share and discuss, redraft and 'publish' their stories. Saxe *et al.* (1993) look at peer interaction and the development of mathematical understandings through cooperative learning, and how the use of insight into peer processes within cooperative learning structures influences student motivation and achievement. Levine (1993), in her chapter on learning English in multilingual classrooms, discusses the effect of teachers' perception of the social composition of their racially and ethnically mixed classrooms. The 'pedagogic space' will clearly differ if this is seen as threatening or as full of liberating potential for socially egalitarian relations in support of learning. Evans (1993), in the light of Vygotsky's own work with 'problem children' as well as with children of all abilities, examines its implications for special education and the current inclusion debate, while Vygotsky's (1978) stress on the importance of play for cognitive development has led play therapists to revise both their technique and understanding of play (Alvarez and Phillips 1998).

Vygotsky's emphasis on the importance of such understanding for teachers to be able to create a successful learning environment both in the special needs field and for children in general has obvious implications for staff development, since it has also afforded the opportunity of 'perceiving the learning difficulties experienced by children with special needs as potentially highlighting problem areas in teaching and learning in general, which need to be addressed for the benefit of all' (Mongon and Hart 1989, Hart 1996). One such problem area clearly relates to how to attend to children's emotional needs.

Emotional factors in learning

There now exists a rich field of knowledge and understanding of children's emotional growth, of the processes of social interactions and relationships which influence it, and of the part these play in enhancing or impeding the capacity for learning (see Greenhalgh's comprehensive account (1994) of the wealth of knowledge available). Not all of it has been made sufficiently available to teachers. Most of them, however, will be aware that *what* children are being taught and *how* they are being taught is of at least equal importance in children's learning, and that attention paid to their feelings and social experiences which matter to them stimulates their learning. But teachers' opportunities to do so have been severely reduced in an over-competitive teaching climate (cf. Warnock (1996) airing widespread concerns).

There is then a tension between what teachers know to be important for the *process* of learning and the perceived official emphasis on its measurable *content*. Working conditions seem to impede their capacity to act in the best interest of their charges. Constantly changing priorities and uncertainties cumulatively seemed to conspire against their professional task. Staff support initiatives have therefore been concerned with enhancing teachers' professional capacities under these difficulties and suggesting that what professionals need is 'a learning environment which accepts anxiety and uncertainties and promotes thinking and understanding' to optimise their resources (Woodhouse and Pengelly 1991, also Hanko 1993a).

Trying to understand children's emotional learning needs and what is involved in the task of meeting them has occupied workers in a range of professions and disciplines. Philosophers accept an education of the emotions as forms of cognition, involving knowledge and understanding (Peters 1974). Psychologists and psychoanalytical therapists agree that the link between emotions and motivation is not a mere linguistic coincidence. As Bennett's findings (1991) in relation to Vygotsky's theory demonstrate, the give-and-take experience of heightened motivation in a group that learns together, with each other and with a teacher aware of its importance, provides a positive feeling of belonging, of being valued. It develops children's confidence as learners and affects their sense of self-worth. Bowlby writes about the 'secure base' which children need, to 'learn without fear' (1988, see also Barrett and Trevitt 1991). Bion (1962, 1970) develops the theory of learning that comes from the experience of 'thinking about feelings', of 'liberation into conceptualisation' that comes from children having their 'unbearable' feelings – such as defiance and hatred – understood by a 'containing' adult who, empathising with what the child may be thinking and feeling, shows him that he is being appreciated, and thereby transforms the 'unbearable' into more manageable, thinkable ones. Mental development is thus seen as deriving from thinking through 'being thought about'. Similarly, Winnicott (1965) shows how a tentative verbalisation of a child's difficult feelings can be a sign to him of the adult's attempt to understand his 'own version of his existence'. (We will see in Chapter 3 how jointly exploring a case like Tony's (pp. 19–24) facilitated his teacher's ability to use these insights to optimum effect).

When Bloom (of taxonomy fame) commented on the importance of affective objectives in teaching and their erosion from course practice in face of the cognitive bias in school testing, he ascribed this erosion to the mistaken 'assumption that the affective would develop without teaching' (cited in Watkins 1996). This, we now know, is indeed erroneous and many teachers now use approaches that set out to attend to the affective/social dimension. Among these are Circle Time (Mosley 1993), Circles of Friends (Newton and Wilson 1996) and the No Blame Approach to Bullying (Maines and Robinson 1991, 1992), which lead children to experience each other as valued members of a group by learning to support and empathise with others in their difficulties. These are liberating experiences that help to create a good learning environment.

Many children's school experiences, however, lead to *dis*affection. A UNISON survey (Special Children, May 1998) reported deep-seated feelings of rejection, of being ignored, ridiculed, even of just not being encouraged in their efforts. Interviews with truants show their perception of school as 'controlling regimented environments' with unsupportive teachers making it hard to return to school ('I felt all the teachers were extremely sarcastic', 'I didn't feel any of them wanted to help me'). Devlin (1997) was told of similar regrets by prisoners when she asked about any particular features in their lives that might have made a difference, while a Social Exclusion Unit report (Archer 1998) comments on some of the reasons given as to why children drop out of education: that school is experienced as boring, too difficult, not leading anywhere.

Thus, school experiences matter. How children experience school, however, has also much to do with the experiences they bring into it. Their self-image may already be so dented that learning anything seems to them an impossible task (as it did with a little Year 3 boy who exclaimed through tears that he 'will never manage' [as he] 'was *born* stupid'). Others have become similarly discouraged, convinced that nobody likes them ('so what is the point of trying?'), joining the ranks of those who 'do not respond even to praise' (Hanko 1994). Anxieties arising from difficulties experienced in their private lives will carry over and affect their work and interactions at school, may remain hidden or may be displayed as problem behaviour, and easily provoke negative responses in their teachers who are then faced with their own emotional vulnerability. Having to deal with their own negative feelings when it matters to be seen as 'in control', they may respond, not with their trained 'professional self' (Kahn and Wright 1980), but with their 'personal kneejerk' self; may add their own anger to the child's; and, at that moment, will not be able to offer that emotionally supportive environment, that 'secure base', in which it becomes possible to explore and 'to learn without fear'.

If we can accept that to be able to create a good learning environment teachers also need for themselves such 'a learning environment which accepts anxiety and uncertainty and promotes thinking and understanding' (Woodhouse and Pengelly 1991), how can a structure of continuing professional development help to bring this about?

Chapter 2

Collaborative Consultation

Continuing development of competence

Examining different models of pedagogic practice, Daniels discusses the concept of a Responsive Pedagogy as a basic requirement for all education. Capable of responding to learners, it 'treats teaching as a competency to be continuously developed... informed by learning, and learning that is informed by the right kind of teaching' (1996) in response to the learner's needs. Finding ways of supporting its development is therefore seen as urgent.

Collaborative problem-solving approaches have been advocated in support of developing such responsive competence. Doubts about their large-scale introduction in schools have, however, been raised, under the assumption that to be feasible certain preconditions are required. For institutions unused to a professional culture of dialogue and sharing of experience and expertise, the number of obstacles raised is legion. They are seen in the degree of interprofessional sharing skills that these approaches require, impeded by status hierarchies and professional rivalries (heightened by proposed legislation on 'performance-related pay' via assessment by 'results'); that shortage of time (excessive workload and administrative pressures) with consequent stress prevent both reflective action in the classroom as well as opportunities for meetings with colleagues; and teachers may deny having difficulties, fearful of having their professional competence questioned or being thought to be in need of 'improvement', or are just innovation-weary, due to too many 'hero innovators'.

If we accept a good learning environment as being one where 'teaching as a competency' is continuously further developed, then the presence of any of these obstacles must be seen as a challenge to its creation. From an interactional systems perspective, Osborne (1998) describes a good learning culture as 'one whose boundaries are robust enough to offer reasonable security to those working within it, yet these boundaries are permeable ... such an open system would be willing to receive and consider new ideas to accept and cope with change'. She refers in this context to the great deal of consultative work with teachers taking place in the schools, which shares these principles, especially as 'attention is paid to the context of the whole classroom group and to the nature of the teacher pupil interaction, including the teachers understanding of their own reactions to ... difficulties' (Osborne 1994).

Creating a good learning environment: the concept of consultation and its practice in schools

It would be a contradiction in terms to demand an absence of problems as a precondition for setting out to create a good learning environment. Accepting the above problems as real, a consultatively collaborative problem-solving approach is geared to addressing them. Those aiming to offer it therefore need to take account of the psychological and institutional difficulties which are likely to militate against its acceptance or implementation.

The principles of this approach have been formulated by pioneers of group consultation such as Balint (1956) for the medical profession and Caplan (1970) for professionals in social work and teaching, followed by relevant accounts from individuals practising the approach in a variety of school settings (see Skynner 1974, Dowling and Osborne 1994, Hanko 1987, 1995) and through LEA behaviour support services adapting problem-solving approaches to whole-school settings. Working with groups of teachers, they interpret their role in various ways, such as 'engaging colleagues in [general] joint problem-solving' or as 'helping teachers to develop their responses to [specific problems like] emotional and behavioural difficulties' (DfEE 1997c).

Consultation has become a well-defined concept in contexts like mental health in which it is useful 'to consider jointly' and 'to take counsel'. Steinberg (1989) describes it as a joint exercise in problem clarification and problem-solving, which enhances the professional competence of those engaged in the process of consultation as well as helping them to learn how to consult with others.

Thus, consultation is here seen not as a process in which a professional acts as *sole* expert who provides others with solutions. Instead he acts as a non-directive facilitating fellow professional skilled in the art of sharing his experience and expertise in a process of joint exploration of a problem. Such collaborative exploration encourages others to develop their own sharing capability in a problem-solving framework, to address existing problems as well as those that may yet arise.

These skills include maintaining one's fellow professionals' autonomy by enabling them to make free and informed choices about how to address a specific problem, and to generate an atmosphere in which they can work together with equal but differing expertise, engaged in a process of developing understanding and skills concerning a third party (such as pupils). The facilitating consultant does *not try to supplant* the others' expertise but *supplements* it, thereby helping to highlight the underlying issues, to find their own workable alternative solutions. The atmosphere is that of a 'work group' (Bion 1961), committed to exploring an agreed issue, unimpeded as far as possible by hidden agendas such as leadership issues (Bion's 'basic assumptions' through which groups may wish to avoid tackling the task note how this threatened to happen for instance in Dipak's case discussion, pp. 45–8).

Where consultation focuses on creating a good learning environment through attending to the emotional and social factors in all children's learning, as it does in this text, it is effective first to explore with teachers those children they find more difficult to teach and what they find most difficult about teaching them. While this focuses attention on the child's behaviour and situation, it also takes into account the teachers' perception of the difficulty and its effects on them, such as erosion of confidence, loss of objectivity, accepting that such children provoke strong feelings about them when they fail to respond to their best efforts. Accepting how difficult it can be, even for trained professionals, not to let such feelings interfere with their responsibilities, such exploration can also highlight how much more difficult such control will be for children with emotional and related social difficulties. They are likely to experience feelings they find difficult to bear, which impede their learning. But their difficulties may be lightened, and their learning enhanced, if an understanding of these feelings can be conveyed to them interactionally by those adults significant in their lives. (Teachers, of course, so often underestimate how important they are for every child in their classrooms.)

This model of consultancy is not prescriptive but points towards workable alternatives. The teacher retains control over the problem and decides how to use his own extended understanding and skills with the child in question and ultimately in any other learning situations.

These crucial aspects of the educational process suggest the Caplan model (1970) of consultative staff development as particularly appropriate since it focuses on maximising the teachers' own resources to deal with a problem, without giving advice which may be perceived as implying criticism of their methods or suggesting these to be insufficient. Chapter 3 shows how this enabled teachers to take a fresh look at the situation and to discover their own ways of improving it, offering them an experience of heightened professionalism in consequence. The supportive structure of the model allows teachers to use those approaches which best suit their way of working, to examine these in relation to the educational task, and to gain for themselves a better understanding of their significance. This cognitive element of the model enables teachers to transfer the understanding and skills gained to other children and situations and to become enagaged in cooperative self-improvement. The method is particularly suitable for teachers in view of their role and their institutional setting, enabling them in their turn to reinforce and extend those aspects of a school's climate that encourages dynamic teaching and an ethos committed to ensuring a good learning environment.

Introducing a consultative problem-solving framework as part of a professional development plan

Schools in the process of establishing a professional development structure tend to be interested in the *training* element of a consultative problem-solving framework. Where the model is based on a learning enhancing case discussion approach (as it is in this text), its training element consists of broadening the discussions of specific cases by highlighting underlying issues in such a way that the child's teacher(s) as well as the whole group – whether or not they all know the child – learn a problem-solving approach which they can apply to meeting other and future problems and needs as they may arise. When introducing the approach to a school, a brief account of its principles and practice (for detail see Part III) needs to specify its aims, immediate and long-term objectives and training procedures. Such specification would offer

- a statement of its overarching *aim*
  - to enhance teachers' competence through collaborating effectively with colleagues
  - to experience how, through sharing and thus maximising their expertise, they can contribute to each others' and their own effectiveness;
- a statement of immediate and long-term *objectives*, such as in this text
  - to sharpen insight into emotional and social factors in learning and failure to learn
  - to develop the skills required to use that insight during an ordinary teaching day, i.e. as an integral part of their professional task;
- a summary of *consultative enablement skills*

as being first and foremost *language communication* skills, i.e. based on an awareness of how communication processes become effective, how one can prevent them from becoming counter-productive or remain ineffective.

This is likely to lead to a more detailed discussion of such skills, which may then be introduced as becoming aware of how

- to convey appreciation of colleagues' experience and expertise in the sharing process
- to share one's own expertise so that it can be of immediate and long-term use
- to develop sharing skills which supplement expertise (i.e. do not seem to want to supplant it)
- not to make a colleague feel worse by seeming to imply that others can handle things better
- to recognise strengths, tap untapped skills and know how to build on them.

In this way a climate conducive to mutual support, respect and commitment can be developed, favourable to collaborative enhancement of competence across the curriculum and ability range. The training group itself can then be introduced to these skills as consisting of:

- the art of asking genuinely explorative, non-judgemental questions (which in themselves can widen insights about a difficulty);
- noticing (e.g. in the answers to such questions) colleagues' strengths on which to build;
- generating, through such give-and-take, information that can help to further highlight the issues underlying the difficulty that is being explored.

Extending a staff's supportive sharing capacities in these ways means that the school is engaged not only in supporting its staff over immediate concerns, but is also engaged in its own continuing professional development.

Chapter 3

Teachers Using Collaborative Consultation in their Schools: Examples of Case Discussions

These school-based case discussions with groups of teachers will show how the participants increasingly felt that they could respond more appropriately to the children whose needs they were exploring, and discovered how they might, by educational means, improve their situation and those of other children with similar problems, as well as adapt the planned curricular programme, ordinary classroom procedures and relationships in such a way that it became an enriched learning experience for the whole class.

The examples are selected because of the range of problems encountered by teachers everywhere, and also to demonstrate how work in the groups developed in their varying primary or secondary school settings. They also show how both the situations presented and the solutions attempted are equally relevant to primary and secondary schools (some junior schools had actually invited to their meetings colleagues from their neighbouring infant school and intake staff from the nearest secondary school they were 'feeding').

The detail offered shows the step by step exploration of issues as workable solutions began to offer themselves, both for the child under discussion and as part of the problem-solving framework that developed in consecutive sessions and on which the consultative process is based. No attempt was made to categorise the children who could have been variously labelled as quiet, withdrawn, fearful, gifted but underachieving, work-refusing, disruptive, rebellious, difficult, hyperactive, attention-seeking, slow learning, with a range of symptoms; nor was there any attempt to classify their behaviour, or to offer clinical diagnoses. That is to say, no decisions were made for the teachers, they were not encouraged to perceive the children solely in terms of their difficulties. We focused instead on the context of the teacher's concern and the problems with which the child's reactions confronted him. What produced negative or positive responses to the day-to-day teaching programme? How do the child and the others in the class relate to each other? How do they receive praise and reprimand, react to success and the lack of it? What positive experiences might it be possible to design for children too discouraged to respond to praise? What is known about the child's out-of-school situation, his siblings, other adults one might be able to enlist in partnership?

In other words, the children's differing reactions were noted in the learning context, to explore what these seemed to indicate about their expectations of others and their view of themselves, about the past experiences which can produce such expectations, and about the new learning experiences which might favourably amend expectations and extend the children's view of themselves and of others relating to them.

All names are fictitious, and identifying detail has been omitted.

Creating a good learning relationship at critical moments

(i) A case of exreme withdrawal – a teacher at a loss how to help an extremely withdrawn child to participate more actively in the work of the class

Ivan

Mr K, Year 6's class teacher, presented the case of Ivan with whom he 'couldn't do anything' while 'all the others responded so well' to his teaching. He had 'tried everything to draw him in', but 'even praise didn't help'.

This primary school staff group had already met a couple of times. They had been made aware of the potential that lies in exploring non-judgementally the context of a pupil's difficulty as briefly described by their colleague. The basic consultative exploration skills had been explained as

- asking 'answerable' questions in such a way that they may widen insights about the pupil's difficulties; and
- noting possible strengths in the teacher on which to build.

The questions they might like to ask would obviously be based on their own expertise and experience with difficult-to-teach children but should not suggest the questioner's own view about how the situation should be dealt with.

When Mr K presented the difficulties he had with Ivan's withdrawn behaviour, the group seemed to sense their colleague's despondency about not being able to help this boy. So, how did they shape their enabling questions? Here was a teacher, disheartened about a seemingly unresponsive child. How had he managed to find something to praise? This first question, directed at a despondent colleague's attempt at using his professional expertise, produced information about Ivan's unexpectedly imaginative writing which Mr K discovered when taking the children's work home to mark. Delighted that he had something to praise him for the next morning, Ivan was however 'back in his shell'. The group then proceeded with questions about the context in which the writing had been stimulated. Was there anything in the content that might offer a message about the child's usual behaviour and the contrast with his unusual response, i.e. tell us something about the boy's 'teachable self' (Oakeshott, 1973)? On hearing that the class had been asked to write about Kipling's 'Just so' story which Mr K had read to them, and that the story was called 'How the hedgehog got his prickles', the group drew a deep breath, and so did Mr K! There was this prickly boy, seeming to fence himself off against the outside world, but who could identify, at least momentarily, with an animal that did just that.

Away from the demands of having constantly to attend to the hundred-and-one interactions and happenings teachers have to take note of in every lesson, and the increasing pressures which they feel lessen their opportunities 'to hear the voice of the child' (Collins 1998, Davie *et al.*, 1996), Mr K was able to benefit from the joint exploration with his group of supportive colleagues, which allowed him to look at the situation in a new light. His professional expertise had been respected, and it was left to him to see how he might use the insights that had developed in the discussion.

At a later session he told us how he had developed the animal project of which the hedgehog story had been a part, into a lesson on language development! Talking about the means with which 'mother nature' has equipped her creatures to defend themselves against danger but how human beings have the means of language to deal with enemies can inspire language activities on resolving conflicts, forming relationships, developing friendships and dealing with any encounters that may occupy children's minds. Keeping Ivan in mind as the unobtrusively 'targeted' child, Mr K was able to offer the whole class a much enriched curriculum.

Ivan's difficulties were of course too complex to be cured just by an enriched curriculum which might, however, help his resilience and the coping abilities (Rutter 1991) to meet the tasks that may yet await him. He did gradually take a slightly more active part, enjoyed the other children's interest in his work when it was displayed, taking an interest in theirs in return. When told, his parents were pleased about this, but had not, it seems, appreciated that there had been a problem. They had always been more concerned about the needs of his older brother, away in a residential school for physically handicapped children. This, too, was a lesson for the group. We shall return to the issue of home–school and interagency communication in a later section.

(ii) An angry ten-year-old boy – reacting to a ten-year-old boy's angry outburst

Progressively each case underlined for the teachers the obvious basics for understanding our interactions with those we experience as difficult-to-teach, that –

- children's difficult behaviour is a reaction to situations they perceive as difficult, influenced by emotions that are linked to other experiences in their lives;

that –

- how we respond to that behaviour will further influence theirs, which, in turn, will influence ours;

and that –

- it is the adult's response which determines whether the interaction will become a virtuous or a vicious circle.

It is thus a question of a teacher's awareness of both perspectives, an awareness which we may have on reflection, but not quite so easily in difficult teaching situations when we have to think on our feet, react in front of 30 or more others who want – and need us – to be in full control. Provoked or despondent, we are faced with our own emotional vulnerabilities, with all those negative feelings which such pupils make us have about them when we do not recognise what anxieties they may be bringing into the school. As the case discussions show, a mutually supportive staff development structure that promotes insight 'interactionally' through shared conceptualising reflection, can help us to apply it at critical moments, when quick appropriate responses are the mark of the professional who has his wits about him when it matters most. Claxton (1997) refers to this as 'implicit know-how' validated by the ongoing reflection.

A good example is one teacher's encounter, described by her colleague, with a ten-year-old in a state of extreme aggressiveness and anger directed at his teacher. She managed to react to the child's angry façade not with anger of her own which would only have added her anger to his and make things worse, but understood it as an outward sign of underlying distress (Graham and Hughes, 1995). She conveyed her concern by telling him how sorry she was that he was feeling so bad, asking him whether there was something that was making him very sad, whereupon the boy burst into tears.

Thinking about and conceptualising as 'reflective practitioners' what this teacher's 'implicit knowhow' conveyed to them, the group suggested a number of things, such as an understanding that

- attacks like these come from unhappy children;
- the attacks were not directed personally at this teacher who only stood in for all other adults who may have contributed to the child's unhappiness;
- she was 'containing' the child's anger, something he had not yet learnt how to do for himself;
- she helped him to understand his own feelings a bit better, such as the link between sadness or anxiety and anger (it is not a chance happening that both share the same linguistic root!);
- experiences like this would allow him to feel that he was, after all, capable of enlisting an important person's concern for him, perhaps beginning to see himself as someone worth caring about by a person significant in his life, rather than feeling 'written off'.

(iii) A hostile fourteen-year-old girl – reflecting on how to respond to her hostility

It is one of the features of collaborative consultancy that it stimulates task-enhancing reflections about issues like these which exert such a powerful effect on teachers' competence and job satisfaction. Teachers not only tend to underestimate their significance in the lives of their pupils but show disbelief that they are having any effect when a child's overt behaviour may at first not appear to improve, as happened in some of our discussions. Research with parents in their mid-twenties who had grown up in children's homes and who at secondary school had given their teachers cause for concern (Quinton and Rutter 1987), has shown how frequently these young people retrospectively ascribed their later resilience in dealing with the hazards and dilemmas of life to some good experiences at school, provided by understanding teachers. These teachers had given them 'the experience of some form of success, accomplishments or just pleasure in activities at school ... rather than just success in formal examinations', which had developed their 'feelings of self-esteem and self-efficacy' (Quinton 1987). Those effects had however been so subtle that the teachers had remained unaware of them.

Becoming aware of such subtleties is part of the task-enhancing reflections that take place in a collaborative consultation group. An example of the effect which a single question arising from such explorations can have on a teacher–pupil relationship was provided by a pastoral care tutor who attended an institute-based training course on collaborative staff development. In a workshop session she had presented her difficulties with a disaffected 14-year-old, unapproachable in her hostility towards the staff, including her tutor, who was at a loss how to help. When the tutor told the group that she was aware of clearly difficult home circumstances, a member of the group asked whether the girl herself was aware of her tutor's concern about those difficulties at home? The tutor thought not, not wanting to seem intrusive, but reported at a later session how, when passing the girl in the corridor the next day, she had briefly stopped, asking whether 'things are still quite difficult at home? We must have a chat some time'. Three days later, this seemingly hostile girl had hesitantly reminded her that 'we haven't had that chat yet'. A feeling of 'having been thought about', of 'being kept in mind' by a supportive adult, had clearly helped to start creating for the girl a better learning environment within which to make progress.

Improving learning situations in a variety of school settings and at different stages in the life of a group

In much of his work Rutter stressed that teachers, like other professionals, can 'cultivate the skills to protect children from unpromising situations [and] help to provide benevolent environments' (Rutter 1991). As the following examples will show, it is possible to 'cultivate' consultative competence also where the group contains members of other schools than their own (or where the settings are multiprofessionally inter-institutional ones to which we will turn in detail in Chapter 7).

A teacher facing a child in turmoil about his mother in prison

Teachers in any kind of school may suddenly be confronted with a child in turmoil and may be unsure how to react. It certainly worried Mrs A when she faced the changes in Tony.

Tony

'Something terrible is happening in my class with Tony; can we – please! – talk about him today?' was the first remark in the group session. As in other schools in this multi-problem city area, the staff of Tony's school (a junior school) and of the adjacent infant school were meeting weekly to discuss, with me as an outside consultant, how best to work with those children whose behaviour caused them concern. This was their fourth meeting, and they had intended to explore another child's case, but their colleague implored them to make time for Tony. In view of this urgency they agreed to try and discuss two cases in this session, giving about 45 minutes to each.

Mrs A briefly told the group that nine-year-old Tony had been a sound learner, most helpful with other children and a splendid member of the class. She had always found it easy to have a good relationship with him. She knew that he and his older brother were brought up by his father and paternal grandparents who seemed to be out of touch with his mother. The school had heard that his mother had been imprisoned many years previously, and was full of admiration for the father and grandparents for the caring home that they provided and the very active, busy life that they led which gave the boys plenty of stimulation through many events and entertainments.

In the previous week, however, during the class's news period, the children's talk had turned from a news item on 'Thieves Caught Red-handed' to the question of whether such people should or should not be sent to prison. Tony had then suddenly got up, told the class that his Mum had been sent to prison many years ago, and that he did not know whether she was still there or whether she was dead. He then sat down, white and silent for the rest of the afternoon, but from the next day had turned into a 'demon' in class and playground, constantly interfering with other children. He was now an unmanageable troublemaker, after having previously been 'mature for his age'. The teacher, disturbed at this transformation, told the group how she had been trying to cope by keeping the whole class as busy as she could so that there would be no chance for anybody to mention what Tony had told them. As she was saying this, however, she interrupted herself, suddenly wondering whether her own frantic busyness was perhaps similar to what was happening at Tony's home all the time, with everybody trying to keep the children's minds occupied with other matters in order to 'protect' the children. She wondered what was the right thing to do? Should she just go on trying to manage Tony somehow, hoping that it would all eventually die down? What was Tony wanting her to do?

In the discussion which followed, the group was guided to focus on the stress felt separately by the child *and* by the teacher. Was it possible to share the stress *with* the child? He had, after all, been close to his teacher beforehand. Had the event not been a communication of something which nobody seemed able to share with him but which was bound to dominate his thoughts? Had his outburst also led to the loss of a necessary barrier, which he now did not know how to do without and perhaps needed to restore? Were his feelings and anxieties now complicated and intensified by having given away the 'family secret' to the whole world? Was there any way in which the teacher could show that she understood all this, without intruding any further, and in which the child could be left to make use of the teacher's understanding? Would it perhaps be possible, eventually, also to convey to the father how important it was for children to be allowed to talk about a missing parent and to think well of her?

Mrs A was left with these questions in mind, and the group turned to their second case. She had found the discussion helpful and was relieved that others had been able to share her anxieties about Tony. A fortnight later she reported that, two days after the discussion, she had managed to find a good moment, after 'another awful day with Tony', to have a quiet talk with him. She had told him that she had noticed how differently he had been behaving lately, how difficult all this was for everybody, how it had all started after he had told them about his Mum and how worried he probably was about it all. She had said that she understood what he must be feeling, and that if he wanted to talk to her about it, she would always have time for him, but that if he did not want to, that would be alright, too. Since then, his troublesome behaviour had ceased. He had not accepted her invitation to talk, but was again relating well to her and to the other children.

We could have left it at that, had the purpose of the group been merely to give teachers an opportunity to get together to share their problems about dealing with specific cases. However, more is required if such case-focused analysis is to aid a training process in which insights gained about a specific case can be conceptualised to become part of a framework for dealing with similar problems as they arise. Such conceptualisation was attempted in this group by inviting the teachers to examine in depth Tony's disturbing behaviour and its termination.

It was suggested to the group that the cessation of the boy's troublesome behaviour, and his more relaxed way of relating to others afterwards, seemed to show that he felt understood and that he had needed his feelings to be acknowledged. It seemed that the teacher had managed to help him to 'reach back over the gap of his breakdown and forward to renewed good relationships', as has been described in other similar cases (Winnicott 1965). Intuitively, the teacher had understood his aggressive behaviour as a sign of panic, and his interference with the work of other children – stopping them from functioning – as a message of distress. She was helped to see both as representations of 'traumatic – unthinkable – experience at an early age' (Dockar-Drysdale 1973), triggered off by the stimulus of the news period on prisons. She had also realised, as she presented the case, how sheltering children from talking about troubling events such as the loss of a parent, as both she and Tony's family had tried to do, may have more to do with the adults' own needs than with those of the children.

This intuitive understanding of the incident and its causes had been shared in the consultation and been thought through in detail, which led to tentative but systematic reformulation of the problem. The earlier build-up of an apparently mature 'false self' and its breakdown were noted, together with the hope of being understood which was shown by acting out the 'unthinkable anxiety' in antisocial behaviour. The teacher's tentative verbalisation of the child's feelings had been a sign to him of her attempt to understand his 'own version of his existence' (Winnicott 1965); she had shown her ability to accept his unthinkable anxiety, and to make it thinkable by sharing it, while setting limits to his acting out his feelings in antisocial ways. She had also shown willingness to help him to face these feelings by expressing them in a safe relationship, but only if he wanted to do so. His message was received and accepted, his despair and his hope had been noted, and it was left to him to decide whether to engage in further communication or to rebuild whatever barrier he needed. She had facilitated the 'spontaneous processes of self-repair' (Winnicott 1965), while stopping short of an interpretive approach, which lies beyond the range or scope of the teacher.

In the group discussions the teachers experienced what Bion (1970) described as 'liberation into conceptualisation', when intuition (the teacher's) is shared and further knowledge applied to each detail, facilitating the search for workable solutions. Tony's case helped the teachers to realise how the apparent maturity of a child's false self can induce us to accept the surface for the whole person, leaving us at a loss to understand 'unintelligible' behaviour changes. The example also suggested that to react to surface behaviour symptoms by attempting to make them disappear without understanding what need they expressed would have been likely to increase the underlying need, even if the symptoms could have been suppressed.

In Tony's case, one could also point out that more was probably being achieved than a desirable short-term result, as has been suggested by others (Wolff 1969, Rutter 1981) and that – apart from helping the child to contain an acutely poignant experience – such on-the-spot yet unobtrusive help during a crisis uses a time of particular receptivity to help aid further understanding. This may also strengthen the child's coping capacities for the future (Quinton 1987), since he experiences – as did the teachers in the group – that one can 'deal with one's life problems by one's own efforts and with the help of others – and a repertoire of learned skills for solving them' (Caplan 1982). The teachers gained in skill through learning that one can help disturbed children to understand and to express their feelings (or, as in this case, to hear them expressed), so that they themselves change their behaviour as a result of understanding themselves better.

Lastly, the group was asked to turn their thoughts to the father. Could more be done for Tony and his brother, if he could be helped to understand that Tony, like other children who live with only one parent, may need to talk about his absent mother, to understand and think well of her and to gain some access to the reality of her existence and that this will help him to cope with otherwise 'unthinkable' anxieties and fantasies? As clinical evidence shows (Bowlby 1979), support like this can make a great difference to both lone parent and child. We took into account how distressed the father would be, if he had heard about the incident, at having the family secret spread all over the school through Tony's outburst. However, there was also evidence of the strength with which he cared for his sons. It was again left to Mrs A's discretion to see whether it was possible to involve the father without thereby adding to Tony's problems.

Summary

To sum up, Mrs A had started the session with a question of how best to help a child's crisis behaviour which was sparked off by ordinary everyday classroom activity. The discussions in the group made a difference to Tony and to Mrs A who had herself become anxious about his behaviour change. She, too, had found that her anxieties could be shared and carried professionally, her strengths could be recognised, her concerns accepted and her reactions put into objective perspective. Understanding was deepened in the whole group as issues were highlighted in joint exploration, so that suggestions for appropriate action arose from the teachers' own growing insight, instead of being imposed from outside. The teacher's decision was part of her expertise and clarification. She had seen Tony's disturbing behaviour as an invitation to act, which she then managed to do in her own effectively tentative way.

Having to solve problems like these can be a burden for teachers who have rarely learned during training not only to be aware of how children's family situations may adversely affect their progress at school but also to use such understanding in their relations with the children and in sensitive parent–teacher partnerships to enhance the children's progress. Mrs A, like her colleagues, had found their joint analysis of these issues thought-provoking, and considerations like these became a feature of their later case discussions, as we shall see when we rejoin them in their concern for Dave and Jeanie below. First we turn to two very different groups and their earliest case explorations.

Two examples of first case discussions

The nature and extent of the difficulty which groups present in their first cases will be influenced by the way that support has been initiated and membership has been recruited, and by how hopeful or dubious they are about its value.

Teresa

Teresa's case was presented in a group of secondary school teachers, all of whom were heads of houses or year tutors. The group was organised by the deputy head, who had heard of such groups working well in other schools in the area. At the first meeting, Teresa was described as an 'anti-authority problem', aggravated by the school's well-intentioned efforts to enlist the father's help, which had misfired because he always disciplined her severely for any misdemeanour.

Teresa's housemaster told us that she had been reported by several masters for breaking school rules just to get attention; she was a bright girl, but never completed her work with them. She was now in Year 11. She lived with her father, an ageing grandmother (who had both come from India in their adult years), an older brother and a younger sister. All three children attended the same school. The mother had left the family many years ago and now had a new family. Teresa visited her occasionally, but less and less often, as she felt that she was in the way.

Her rule-breaking mainly consisted of slipping out of school during school hours, blatantly in full sight of the master on duty. When challenged, she would refuse to give any explanation; 'like a wall' when reprimanded, she seemed to dare teachers to reprimand her by this open breaking of rules. The more she was reprimanded, the worse she became. When asked to help the school in this matter, the father had insisted that each new incident should at once be reported to him. He would then cane her for it. The teachers had therefore not contacted him again, and he then instructed his son to report on her. He seemed to follow these instructions diligently.

When the group explored the whole situation, they noticed that Teresa (walking out like her mother?) openly defied only men teachers, whom she seemed to manipulate into rejecting and restricting her like her father. The woman teacher in the group, who also taught her, spoke well of her and had been unaware of these difficulties. She had found her quiet in class, always complying, albeit minimally so, and never volunteering to answer any questions. She looked extremely unhappy at times. This teacher then also mentioned that the younger sister, who had just joined the school, was beginning to behave oddly and becoming very attention-seeking.

Encouraged to think about the situation of this adolescent girl, so blatantly rejected by the male members of her family and with no mother to turn to, the teachers agreed that it would be a good idea to give her the opportunity of feeling that men could be on her side. They felt that it might help if the men teachers tried not to be stage-managed into acting as reprimanding guards and to be as accepting and helpful as possible, without expecting an immediate positive response, however. They discussed whether they might not renew their contact with the father more constructively, and might persuade him to accept his daughter's behaviour better, and perhaps to discuss with him how severe punishment often made her behaviour worse. None of us likes to be threatened and we all tend to work more happily when we feel accepted. They also explored how they might help Teresa to cope with her situation, thought of elements in the curriculum which could give pupils in general a deeper understanding of how human beings relate within different societies and generations, and of the various ways that people find to deal with them.

At a follow-up meeting two terms after the end of this group's one-term course, Teresa's case came up as one of the happiest developments: she had planned to leave both school and home at the end of her fifth year but, unable to find a job, had returned the following autumn. She had begun to confide in one of the men teachers who had been trying to relate to her along the lines that we had discussed. She had told him what a shock it had been to her to see how upset her father had been to learn of her unhappiness and her wish to leave the family home. The teacher had then tried to help her to understand her father's probable feelings, had talked about what loss and separation do to people and had since then noticed in Teresa a striking depth of understanding. She had told him later that 'things are better now at home'. He had also noticed that she was now being met by a boyfriend at the school gates at the end of the day. There had been no recurrence of her challenging behaviour this year.

Although this had been a group's first case discussion, the teachers, in contrast with their earlier reprimanding treatment, had found a way of providing at least some support in this girl's stifled struggle for independence and, judging by what she said and how she changed, had perhaps also helped her to begin to develop the kind of understanding which may enable her to cope with her childhood scars.

They had considered the restrictive role that she had 'made' them play and had examined how they might develop their relationship with a 'hopeless' parent who seemed to be endangering a pupil's progress, in addition to what helpful learning experiences they might provide for the whole class through skilful use of the curriculum. Remaining cautious about further contact with her father, they had nevertheless been able to help Teresa through acceptance, support and respect for her dignity, to change her reactions to her father's treatment sufficiently for her both to assert herself and to feel for him and also to secure for herself an improvement at home and better relations outside. No doubt she would have found such support even more helpful if relations at home had not improved.

The teachers whom she had so blatantly provoked into dealing with her severely had been enabled to see her aggressive provocations in a different light, had ceased to be provoked, had begun to support her struggling maturity and had helped her to face what was threatening her maturing self. They were able to demonstrate to her that attitude of concern for others through which one can accept 'good' and 'bad' as parts of a whole person and can understand better the needs of those who did not appear to show the same concern. She could do this as her own problems were understood and she was helped to cope with them. It seems to pay dividends on several accounts if teachers take time to listen to pupils, and to each other's experience of them. Teresa's teachers shared their differing experiences of her in a consultative back-up setting in which her responses in different situations and to different teachers – apparently contradictory – took on a new meaning which enabled the teachers to see her in a different light and to help her. This ameliorated her situation both at school and at home, beneficially affected the relationship between child and parent and drew attention to the possible problems of siblings, whose 'oddities' (the sister's symptoms and the brother's uncharitable behaviour) had until then been noted but not been attended to.

It would be naive to think that the difficulties of all pupils from ethnic minorities, straddling such disparate cultural and inter-generational problems, can be similarly resolved, but problems such as Teresa's now confront a good number of teachers, and the provision of at least some authentic support can make a great difference. Teachers can be faced with actual calls for help from their pupils. We heard from a teacher in another secondary school group who told how two Asian girls – bags packed and about to run away from their severely restrictive homes – implored her to help them. In the nursery and infant school, teachers may meet second and third generation 'immigrant' children with emotional problems whose mothers, having rejected their own mothers' foreign culture in adolescence, lack acceptable maternal support now that they are mothers themselves and are struggling with severe depressions. Teresa's teachers have not, I think, just been 'lucky' with their results. There seemed to be grounds for hope that the timely support, which they had at first been unable to give because they did not understand her provocations, may have helped her to cope and care not only in the present, but also in future. (For the practice of pastoral care for Asian girls, see Pelleschi (1985).)

Don

Don was presented at the second meeting of a group of a dozen teachers from three infant and junior schools on one site, later to be joined by secondary school intake staff, and was the third case considered. Two junior school teachers had presented cases of two boys at the first meeting, had begun to try out some of the ideas produced during the discussion, and had reported that the boys had begun to respond to them better already, one being 'now a changed boy'. It seemed necessary therefore for me to sound a note of caution against expecting such sudden changes in every case or mistaking quick changes for permanent solutions. Mrs B then presented the case of this eight-year-old in the top class of the infant school.

She was greatly concerned about his inability to cope at all in class. She said that he did not listen to explanations, was convinced that he 'can't do' whatever she required and, when she coaxed him, would sob for great lengths of time. He wanted her to sit beside him all the time, stopped working if she left him and did not believe her when she said 'I know you can do it'. Although he did not find writing difficult and liked to write in her presence, he wanted to play all the time, which she allowed him to do as far as possible, while feeling very uneasy about giving him special treatment so below his age. The group asked about his background. Mrs B described an all-female home with quite a strong-willed, unsupported West Indian mother who worked outside the home until late in the day. A teenage sister acted as mother substitute and collected Don and his six-year-old sister from school every afternoon. The younger sister was herself very naughty at school and teased her older brother mercilessly in public. It seemed that when he was younger he had been left with child-minders who were unable to meet his early need for play, which would account for his wanting to play now. Thinking about his desolate sobbing, the group were guided to speculate about his possible depression. He was always among seemingly powerful women at home and at school (the school had an all-female staff), and defenceless even against the taunts of a younger sister. Was he getting any support in 'being a boy'? Since there were at least some happier moments during the day when he could succeed (as in his writing), could such situations be multiplied, perhaps through some link with his play? Could he be 'caught at being successful', helped to be helpful and then rewarded with permission to do what he liked best? Could there be some exchange of information, at least occasionally, with his busy mother, to see whether she might be able to find at least a little time daily just for him?

At the end of the meeting, Mrs B confessed her relief that there had been no suggestion of not letting him play but that his play might be linked to learning activities. She now had a number of ideas for this and for some contact with the mother.

A few weeks later, Mrs B reported that Don had begun to respond, and that an exciting additional development had arisen from the first discussion, which involved another member of the group, Mr G from the junior school to which Don would proceed nine months later. Following the discussion of Don's difficulties, this teacher had offered, with the agreement of his headteacher, to meet a small group of boys in the infant school, including Don, once a week for various activities. The offer had been gratefully accepted (and proved such a success that the school decided at the end of the year to fill a vacant post with a male teacher). For Don, that group became the highlight of the week. He became more outgoing in the company of his male peers, started to organise and speed up 'his' group to be in time for Mr G; his progress there was linked with the learning activities in his classroom at which he had hitherto failed.

One result of Don's improvement also led the teachers' group to consider an apparently peculiar feature of classroom dynamics.

Martin

Martin, who had been 'good' when Don was in trouble, now seemed to have taken over Don's role. Other teachers immediately mentioned similar experiences and were encouraged to explore what seemed to be happening in such situations. They were offered some group theory as to how a role which is relinquished by one member of a group will be assigned to another if the group needed someone to carry it. They related this to the dynamics of the class–teacher relationship and asked themselves what parts they might be playing in the constellation of their classes, what the implications were for the management of the situation and how they could help the children to achieve eventual autonomy and the ability to withstand group pressures.

Mrs B then thought that she was herself contributing to this new difficulty in her vexation. There seemed to be a regular sequence. Martin would make an unreasonable demand (e.g. to read to the head teacher at an inconvenient moment); Mrs B would feel that he was trying it on and would answer, shortly, 'no, you can't'. Martin would start upsetting the other children, and she would then try to mitigate her rejection by being nice to him. She had now become aware of her inconsistency and how she had unintentionally kindled the trouble through being irritated by this new difficulty and had then rewarded disruptive behaviour; so she began to find ways of making necessary refusals less total (e.g. she would say, 'You can't read to Mrs M now, but we'll ask her if she can see you when you have finished your bit of writing. It's ever so nice what you have been doing.').

The aim of these discussions was not only to increase the teachers' insight into the cases presented, but also to introduce them to the kind of questions which might enable them to find workable solutions to the problems of the classroom. This requires a certain amount of direction in the early stages. Both groups illustrate how a consultant's initially high profile can start this process, generate ideas in response to a need better understood and lead from the case in question into issues which are important for teaching in general.

In neither case did the directiveness take the form of advice on how to handle the pupil, as the teachers had originally expected. Instead, they were involved in exploring alternatives and in making their own decisions about them. In both groups they accepted, with considerable relief in one case, the consultant's expectation that they would use their own judgement with regard to the questions raised. Both groups were able to appreciate quite soon the possibility of unintentionally reinforcing a child's problematic behaviour by the teacher's own reaction to it. They discovered how to use this self-awareness to good purpose, both in response to a child's immediate need and in the service of long-term educational objectives.

Both cases also had their inter-school aspects, directly so in Don's case where immediate inter-school activity came to benefit him and other children, and as an issue to be considered, at least, in Teresa's case.

How groups develop their competence from case to case

(i) Development of skills in a three-term inter-school primary staff group (from Don and Martin, to Michael to Vic)

Don and Martin

By the end of the first term, the teachers who had been concerned with Don and Martin had accepted that, even with consultation, problems would not go away overnight and had got used to not being advised what to do and to exploring the issues instead, in order to be able to find workable solutions. Although the questions asked by the consultant and colleagues in the group, and the ideas produced in response, tended to be transformed into something like advice, this tendency decreased in the course of the term. The children discussed were no longer presenting the teachers with 'insoluble' problems, and the group finished the first term on such an optimistic note that they invited another infant school, whose children proceeded to one of the junior schools already represented, to join them.

Michael

Michael's teacher, Mrs C, belonged to this fourth school, which had not, like the others, actually asked for help with disturbed children but had gladly accepted the invitation to join the group.

The issue of seemingly unhelpful parents and home situations had come up in most of the cases discussed. It complicated Michael's case in a different but equally poignant way. After attending a few of these discussions in the group's second term, Mrs C presented Michael: six years old, very anxious in new situations, tearful and panicky at everything that he was asked to do for himself, even if well within his ability, refusing to eat unless Mrs C sat beside him, soiling himself unless she took him to the toilet and scratching other children when they claimed her attention. To the group, his fears and uncertainty about his own adequacy seemed likely to have something to do with the father's lack of time for the family, his disregard of the boy and his preference for the younger sister, which the mother had mentioned to the teacher. The group then discussed whether the child's feelings of self-worth could be enhanced in small steps during the school day and whether the mother, who seemed to let the boy control her by his 'helplessness', might be induced to do likewise.

Mrs C, still new to the group, did not participate in this discussion but listened thoughtfully. As we heard later, she attempted both strategies. She had hesitated for some time to broach the subject with the mother but eventually did so in one of their chats at the school gate, suggesting that it might help Michael if his father could be persuaded to spend about 15 minutes a day playing with him and making him feel important. Although the mother was at first loath to bring the topic up at home, the discussion seemed to have had some effect. A few weeks later, Mrs C told the group that Michael – who had never talked about home at school – had begun to talk to her about his dad, and how he had played football with him. He was also becoming less tense and more self-reliant, all of which seemed to Mrs C like a sort of miracle. She congratulated the mother accordingly.

The following term, however, Mrs C reported that Michael was 'losing his spark'. When she cautiously mentioned this to the mother, she heard that, when she told her husband about Michael's improvement at school, he stopped spending time with him 'since he was all right now!' Mrs C then encouraged the mother to impress on her husband how important he still was for the boy, hoping that this would induce him to give Michael some attention during the coming summer holidays.

In talking about Michael during the spring and summer terms, the group, again, had discussed much more than a sequence of events. The poignancy of the experience made them explore how badly *parents* can underestimate their significance to their children and what *teachers* can do – even in face of initial resistance – to encourage them to support their children more actively. They examined how one also needs to respect the complexities of family relationships and must not push advice. This had helped Mrs C, a newcomer to the group, to become less afraid of 'seeming to pry' and had enabled her to make effective suggestions as she and the mother exchanged information about the child. The group as a whole had shown and commented on their growing self-confidence in seizing opportunities for such exchanges. They found that this often gave results, especially when the problem seemed to be lack of understanding rather than a deeper disturbance in family relationships. Even in more serious cases, parents seemed to gain something from sharing anxieties with the teacher, as we shall see when this group turns its attention to Vic.

It is also of interest that, as a group develop their skills in exploring the underlying issues, newcomers are able to benefit from their earlier explorations and from the questions that the members have learnt to ask themselves, from their awareness and from actions reflecting the stage reached by the group as a whole. (It had been a special feature of this group that, alongside core members attending throughout the course, short-term members attended for half a term, or even once only for special cases, to give as many of the staff the opportunity to attend as wanted to.) Like newcomers, short-term members, as we shall see with Vic's teacher, seemed to catch up quite quickly with the stages of the core group that preceded their arrival. This resembled what workers in the related fields of counselling and psychotherapy report as *special features of brief attendance*, when limited time may encourage a feeling of urgency.

Vic

Concurrently with the summer term follow-up on Michael, Vic's teacher, Miss D, had brought up the difficulties that the school had with this seven-year-old.

Vic had been 'destructive from the first moment that he joined the school' in his third year and 'in trouble every day', 'hated everybody', 'had no interest in anything' and always demanded immediate attention; bright but underachieving, he concentrated only on things that he knew he could do, such as easy first-year work. He had no friends, kicked other children, ripped up work-cards and swore loudly at his teacher, who had 'tried everything' without success and despairingly would now be 'glad to see the back of him'. The mother had moved into the area on remarriage. The stepfather, apparently on good terms with the boy before the marriage and academically ambitious for him, had in the meantime lost patience with him and begun to compare him unfavourably with his own two children, who lived with their mother. He was now treating him severely while his troublesome behaviour grew worse and he began to bully his step-siblings when they met. The school then learnt from the mother that her husband was threatening to leave her unless she got rid of Vic. Most unhappy about this but wanting to save her marriage, she was now wondering whether 'to let Vic go into care'. Things had got so bad between the parents that a child-minding neighbour was now helping to rescue Vic by taking him into her own house, away from the strife.

Vic had first been discussed in the previous term, at an ad hoc meeting with the whole staff of the school. This discussion had helped the teacher that Vic then had to improve the relationship between them, but she had to leave the school and Vic had to adjust to a new teacher. Miss D, an alert, committed, young probationer, had been present at the earlier discussion and could therefore now 'tune in' to Vic's behaviour. However, the child clearly found the change of teacher very upsetting, and a colleague of hers, a core member of the inter-school group on the site, invited her to talk about these difficulties in the group.

Miss D told us how, when Vic refused to work for her, she 'bent over backwards' to help him, even in his worst tantrums, using a strategy of giving in constructively (such as letting him play with the gerbils). She was resentful, however, that her head teacher kept coming into the room to see how Vic was getting on and to tell her to handle him more firmly. As she did not believe in this, she could not make it work. As a result she had begun to hate the whole situation, especially since Vic, having sensed the disagreement between Miss D and the Head teacher, had now begun to ask to move to another class, that of Mrs X. This made Miss D feel even more inadequate and unhappy, both 'hating' Vic for this and feeling like putting her arm round him to comfort him – feelings which the mother had also spoken of when telling the head teacher how Vic was spoiling her marriage. Aware how much Miss D minded Vic's rebuff of her efforts and love, I was able at this point to draw the group's attention to other resemblances between the adults at home and those at school in their relationships with Vic. He had lost a father who, he had once said, 'was better than [his] new Dad' and had lost a teacher who had begun to understand him. Mother and 'new Dad', on the one hand, and the head teacher and Miss

D, on the other, also disagreed on how he should be treated, which, at home, meant rescue by the neighbour; so perhaps Vic was trying to reproduce this solution by asking to move to another teacher's class.

This apparent *re-enactment* by the staff of what was happening at home, and the child's similar response to it, could now be discussed at one of the last meetings, which the head teacher also attended. Seeing it as the far from rare phenomenon of an 'unwitting professional response' (Britton 1981) helped to ensure that there would be no loss of face over the disagreement between colleagues (especially colleagues of such disparate status as the head teacher and a probationary teacher). It was possible first to explore in general the anxieties of committed professionals, irrespective of their length of experience and professional status, when faced with such harrowing cases as Vic's, and how easily these can lead to staff disagreements which may resemble those at home. We then looked at how teachers who become aware that their anxieties reflect those of the children can use this insight to help them to understand themselves better. Miss D could herself give an example of this: she had, in the meantime, had a chat with Vic, explaining that she, too, had sometimes to do as she was told, even if she did not quite want to, and how angry this can make one feel. This seemed to have made a deep impression on him and may have helped him to identify with her. She spoke of a much better relationship with him since then; she was herself more relaxed with him, and he was doing better work and no longer asked to move to another class. All this the head teacher was able to confirm. The head teacher also told the group that she had previously advised the mother to seek help from the child guidance clinic. The mother had already been much helped by the support that she had received from the school following their discussions and no longer wished to send Vic away; she said that she now knew that it was not Vic who needed guidance, but she and her husband. She had therefore contacted the Marriage Guidance Council and already felt that her marriage was beginning to improve.

This case discussion, by an inter-school group whose core members had now met for nearly three terms, demonstrates what consultancy can do for a school both within and across its boundaries.

It shows with what sophistication such a group can approach a child's apparently intractable situation, as they gradually deepen their understanding of such children's needs and of how they can meet these better. Vic, who hated everybody, could nevertheless be seen as in need of benign authority to help him to bear his feelings of anger and depression when threatened with the consequences of his parents' problems. The teachers could be helped to understand his needs better by the support that they themselves received in relation to their own anxieties about the way that they handled him and the way that they worked together as colleagues within the institutional hierarchy and across the school boundaries. Learning not to reproduce the dynamics of a child's home situation, they could give Vic the new learning experiences which he needed and provide enough support to a despairing parent to prevent her making a perhaps irreversible decision (like giving her child into care) out of despair. She was enabled to think again and to seek the kind of help which made such a decision unnecessary.

In this case, too, newcomers to a group (including the secondary school's intake staff), even at this advanced stage of its existence, were able to benefit from the support which the group had developed and the questions that members were asking themselves.

(ii) Development of skills in a two-term inter-school primary staff group (from Tony to Dave and Jeanie (three consecutive case discussions))

As to the phenomenon of re-enactment as an unwitting professional response, the reader is referred to current discussion (Britton 1981) of how difficult it is for professionals to resist such a response and how detrimentally failure to do so affects the help they could otherwise give. As we saw in Vic's case discussion, the processes which can be activated in staff group consultation can contribute to awareness of these issues. This can sometimes develop quite early in the life of a group. Dave's case illustrates another aspect of such unwitting re-enactment; here the pupil's difficult behaviour was reflected in the presentation itself and discussion of his problems.

We now rejoin the staff of Tony's school (see Tony's case, pp. 19–24) as they explore how one might help Dave and Jeanie.

Dave, 'an infuriating boy, who never listens and who cannot even copy from the board'

Dave's case was presented a week after we had discussed Tony's in their fourth meeting. We saw how at the previous meeting the whole group had rallied round Mrs A, had identified with her concern for him and had followed the direction of my 'thinking aloud'. With the exception of the previous session, Dave's teacher, Mr E, had seemed set – through his frequent 'yes, but...' interjections – to become the group's resident 'butter-in', trying to keep the talk at the level of breezy non-concern. With remarks like 'Ah well, that never did me any harm', he would brush aside his colleagues' explorations as irrelevant but now and then throw into the discussion quite harrowing details about early bereavement in his own life. Such personal comments, as we shall see later, cannot be taken up in a professional staff support group, since they are outside its brief and scope. Yet we know that our personal experience can have an effect on our reactions to others and, in the case of a teacher, on his reactions to his pupils and his demands on them. It was with this background in mind that I listened to Mr E's description of Dave.

Eight years old, now in his second term at this school, Dave is exasperatingly 'lazy', always talking to others, the only one in the class who will make a mess of things, who cannot even copy from the board, but who can sometimes surprise by good work. He never listens, just switches off, does the opposite from what he is told and underachieves in everything. Mr E finds it hard to understand, comparing him with his 'hard-working, extremely bright sister' who is one year older – how there can be two such different children in one family? He quotes the mother as confirming that Dave is an infuriating boy, so different from his clever and hard-working sister.

At this point, the group asks for further information, clearly trying to dig for any positive features in Dave that had been hinted at but buried in Mr E's account. When asked about the surprisingly good work, he could not remember, and this lapse of memory made him thoughtful. The group then recalled their own experiences with children who refused to work and how often there seemed to be another child in the family who 'cannot do anything wrong'. They gave examples of how some of their attempts at building up self-esteem seemed to have worked. Mr E, however, countered each example with either 'it wouldn't work with Dave' or 'I've tried all this', and switched off at any good idea offered, unable to listen, making himself, like Dave, the only one in the group who was so different. He eventually induced in the group a feeling of hopelessness, which must have resembled what both Mr E and Dave were feeling in the classroom.

Having so far remained silent in the discussion, I decided not to point this out at this stage. Instead, I used the device of the 'relevant tale' (Caplan 1970), a true example of how fanning small positive sparks in seemingly totally negative behaviour can make a difference. I related an incident from another group of a teacher who, like Mr E, had noticed a tiny potential for better behaviour (Mr E had done this but had only used it to prove that Dave could do better if he tried, as exasperated teachers often do). The teacher of the tale, however, had used this potential in a matter-of-fact manner to give the pupil hope about himself rather than to confirm his despair.

The 'tale' was intended to deflect attention from Mr E at the moment of the group's hopelessness about him and to remind him instead of his own buried awareness of the boy's potential, by illustrating a way out of the vicious circle of perpetual defeat. This lead the group to recall, at the end of the meeting, how they had obtained better results when they had worked on the relationship with a work-refusing child, instead of constantly demanding better work, which had got them nowhere, as with Dave (thus identifying with Mr E as having known failure instead of contrasting their own 'better' results with his, as they had done earlier).

At the next meeting, Mr E almost casually mentioned that he had been trying out one or two of last week's ideas and that Dave surprisingly seemed quite responsive to him this week. He was now showing his own responsiveness to Dave and Dave's response to that, which made Mr E more hopeful about him. This seemed a better moment to comment on last week's parallels between the interaction of the group and Mr E, and the teacher–pupil interaction which he had described – how Mr E had played Dave's part in the group, who thus experienced what it was like to have a Dave in the class and responded to him as if he were Dave, feeling hopeless at his apparent refusal to consider their ideas. This the group found fascinating, especially Mr E who now saw how this had happened, and several times referred to it in later sessions. In one of these he reported laughingly how he had involved another colleague in such discussion when he had caught both himself and the colleague 'fixing' another child inadvertently in his bad behaviour. Equally important, he felt that he was managing to convey something of his greater hopefulness to Dave's mother, who in turn seemed to be becoming more accepting. While Dave was still a problem, it now seemed to him remediable. It no longer aroused feelings of exasperation, as it had done when he had failed to link what had amounted to a form of work paralysis with the hopelessness which Dave must have felt about himself both at home and at school.

This discussion – in sequence – exemplifies the different ways in which a consultant can exercise the role.

In contrast with my somewhat directive involvement during the previous session (Tony's case discussion), I had said very little, apart from using the 'relevant tale', whose functions were to divert attention from Mr E's hopelessness while helping the group to support him – not by recounting their own success stories but by recognising what support potential he might already have, ready to be drawn out by support from others. This helped him to behave likewise with a failing pupil, so that both he and the child had less need to make others feel useless. His report suggested that he had made a beginning in that direction.

As has been found in training groups with doctors (Gosling 1965) and social workers (Irvine 1959), the teacher's 'impersonation' of the pupil evoked his own response in the group, giving them a taste of what it was like to be that pupil's teacher. The consultant tried to help the group to share these feelings and then to overcome them, instead of being overwhelmed, as the teacher had been. In this context the 'relevant incident' was used as a teaching technique.

The case also illustrates the need for carefully timing comments on the reflection of the situation in the classroom. As we shall see later, such timing must depend on the effect that the comments seem likely to have on the discussion. Had I made these comments while Mr E was still feeling helpless they would not have been helpful, as they were when he had become more hopeful and his experience could be looked at as a whole. It was more acceptable to wait until feelings had cooled before drawing attention to what it had felt like for Mr E to be behaving like Dave, and for the group to be getting nowhere, as Mr E was with Dave, and using this to illuminate the problem between teacher and child. As Mr E began to understand and respect the pupil's feelings behind his refusal to work, he could also relax his pressure.

In this way, he and his colleagues found it possible to recognise when their own behaviour was self-defeating, which is notoriously not facilitated by criticism. It was brought about through the group process, which enabled Mr E to relax his hold on his preconceived ideas about Dave and about his own ineffectiveness with him. He could now have a fresh look at the situation, seeing it also from the pupil's point of view, and respond more appropriately to the needs indicated by the boy's behaviour. Only then was Mr E able to make demands on Dave in such a way that the boy could begin to meet them.

Jeanie

The following week, the group discussed Jeanie – a girl in Tony's class – whose difficulties, of growing concern to her teacher, Mrs A, were also involving Mrs A with a social worker with whom she disagreed.

It tends to be the client – in the case of children the child and parents – who suffers when there are such interprofessional disagreements, wounded feelings or attempts to defend challenged competences (see Chapter 7). These hazards could be tackled in good time by Mrs A, who was wondering how to help this nine-year-old in her crippled relationships with others.

Jeanie so irritated everybody with her fussy attention-seeking helpfulness that others found her unbearable and no one in the class wanted to work or play with her. This worsened with every new attempt that she made to be helpful. Fostered since babyhood, but not freed for adoption by her alcoholic mother who met her at irregular intervals, Jeanie seemed happy with her foster parents but frightened that she might become 'mad' like her mother. According to her foster mother, she also feared the frequent visits of the social worker, to whom she could not relate.

The teacher could see that there was a difficulty, as the social worker had not wanted her to discuss Jeanie in our support group or with him, since according to her he did not think that teachers are qualified to deal with such cases. He had apparently told the foster mother that the child should be seen by a psychiatrist, to which the foster mother had reacted with shock, feeling that she had failed Jeanie. She had spoken to Mrs A about this in a frank and caring way, which had strengthened Mrs A's impression that no child could be in better foster care than Jeanie. She had tried to convey this to the foster mother, recalling Jeanie's happy accounts of her relationship with her.

After this account the group was helped to explore whether Jeanie could be guided towards a less obtrusive helpfulness and whether some of the more mature children in the class could be encouraged to be more friendly when working in a group with her. The group were also asked to examine what opportunities there were for foster mother, social worker and school to exchange information in such a way that all sides could listen to each other and explore what Jeanie really needed.

A few weeks later, Mrs A reported that this strategy was beginning work, that Jeanie was responding and that 'a lot was now going for her'. Mrs A also felt that the discussion had helped her to give more support to the foster mother by tentatively exploring with her Jeanie's anxieties and possible feelings of guilt towards her own mother, who wanted to be with her but had to leave her after each brief encounter, and by saying that a caring foster mother such as her was bound to be a tremendous support. She had suggested that Jeanie might like to talk to her foster mother about these things and that it might also be a good idea for teacher and foster mother to include the social worker in their next discussion.

The group then heard that the head teacher of the school was inviting the social worker and the foster parents to meet herself and the class teacher. This enabled the group to consider beforehand the possible implications of the disagreements between teacher and social worker, alerting the teacher to the hazards of interprofessional rivalry and to her opportunity to handle them with sensitivity. Mrs A, encouraged by Jeanie's good response to her strategies, felt that referral to yet another agency seemed inappropriate at this moment, as it might reinforce the child's feeling of being unacceptably different, which was already underlined by the social worker's frequent visits. She therefore decided to suggest that things could be left to tick over for a while; she and the foster parents would see what evolved as they built on the insights gained. Thus the social worker's suggestion of referral would not be rejected but postponed. Mrs A then agreed with the social worker that help through child guidance should be offered after the ground had been prepared, depending on what needs emerged as both home and school worked together along the lines agreed. Social services agreed that their worker's visits might, in the meantime, be less frequent.

All this paid dividends; while the teacher's sensitive attempt to overcome the disagreement between the social worker and herself prevented it from escalating into defensive insistence on premature suggestions from either side, it also heightened the foster mother's confidence in her relationship with Jeanie and it helped Jeanie directly and indirectly. A couple of weeks later, Mrs A reported that Jeanie was now rather more relaxed with the others in her class, had begun to talk to Mrs A about her 'two Mums' and allowed more access to her thoughts and feelings.

In this group, as in others which contain teachers from several schools serving the same community, there also arose a particular benefit as a result of the inter-school setting. Meeting colleagues from other schools (both infant, junior and secondary) in the neighbourhood, they may find that some members of the group have previously taught the child presented or may be teaching one or more siblings and know their parents, so that they may be able to add something about the family situation. When the child's former teachers hear about his problems in the present school and gain increased understanding, they are likely to view some of their present pupils differently or may be able to give some anticipatory guidance before a pupil proceeds to the next school.

In Jeanie's case, her former infant school teacher learnt in the group how the child's difficulties – which the teacher had wrongly hoped she would grow out of – had increased with age; she commented at the end of the discussion that it was clearly not sufficient just to hope for improvements and that unobtrusive help is best given as early as possible. The group process had activated a better understanding of the irritating child and of how easily one provides such attention-seekers with justification for their fears of rejection by rejecting them afresh with each manifestation of their craving for acceptance. The group members also became more aware of how the vicious circle might be broken by paying more attention at an early stage to the desired behaviour.

(iii) Two case discussions of a two-term intra-school secondary staff group (John and Dipak)

Disagreement between professionals occurs, as we know, across as well as within institutions, and can enrich professional life as much as it sometimes frustrates it. Hazards are more likely when there is insufficient exchange of information and no systematic discussion of experience between colleagues – a risk known to most secondary school staffs in particular. Since they have to deal for much shorter periods with the difficulties of many more pupils, they may easily not be aware of how any one pupil's problems assume significantly different manifestations with different teachers. We saw how much better Teresa's teachers understood and began to support her after they had systematically explored the various, seemingly contradictory, experiences that they had with her. Such exchange of unclouded information about a difficult pupil can be particularly useful to both pupil and teachers in the case of those whose aggressive behaviour appears to challenge everything that teachers represent and to refuse even the best-intentioned efforts to help them to progress.

John

John dared his teachers to hit him and threatened to thump them if they did.

He was a mathematically gifted 15-year-old who had managed within 14 months to be demoted from the top mathematics set down to the sixth, doing increasingly less work after each demotion. Promised promotion if he worked hard, he still came bottom in each new set, in spite of the ability that he had shown. He had also become insolent, sneered at teachers when spoken to and was sent out of classrooms because of his aggressive behaviour. However, he did get on well with some teachers, such as the physics mistress, who managed to deflect his behaviour with jocular retorts which he liked, and with two of the men teachers whom he had at first challenged with the same stubborn defiance but to whose firm friendliness he was now responding.

His parents were divorced, the two children split between them, and John lived with his father and stepmother but, when in trouble, secretly sought comfort from his mother, which the father tried to prevent. However, this knowledge alone had not helped the teachers to deal with John constructively.

We therefore focused on the teachers' differing experiences with him and on what his different reactions might suggest about his needs and how to meet them. An important question which arose was whether teachers do not have a choice in how they react to the difficulties that we all experience when we teach rejecting pupils who treat us with aggression and provocation. We looked at how such feelings can develop – how years of parental strife might for instance have set John a bad example as regards the management of aggression and have aroused chaotic feelings with no help in dealing with them. Was John perhaps 'testing' his teachers for their ability to control that chaos, wanting confrontations but needing people to set limits without rejecting him? He seemed to become 'teachable' with teachers who asserted authority firmly but not punitively, whom he could not goad into the aggressiveness which he himself felt towards authority figures and who could see in him not a boy who challenged their authority but a boy who needed their guidance into adulthood, whose 'bluff' they could call jocularly but without ridicule and whose 'reality' they appreciated. Any other responses, such as the retaliation that the other teachers had reported, would feel to him like adult pretence which he had to challenge; where he was not victorious in this way, however, he seemed to be able to settle down quite happily to serious work. This seemed to happen with teachers who refused to confirm his view of himself as an unacceptable person, who passed the test of setting him limits without feeling they had conquered an opponent (Winnicott 1965) but who knew that they had achieved something on his behalf.

The two main questions to consider were how to deal constructively with behaviour like John's and how to do so in the face of severe provocation in public, when one is under pressure to remain in charge.

Could one, for instance, use the time that John forced them to spend in conflict with him differently, talk with him about his anger, show that one understood it and tentatively reflect his feelings back to him, i.e. show him that one accepted his reasons for feeling angry but that he must not act it out, that he, too, sometimes managed to control his anger and that that was an achievement in the right direction? Could one also talk to him about the anger which he incited in others and about how this can make people unfair? Could one make him understand that his own unfairness towards others and theirs towards him were almost inevitable if he went on provoking them? Could he be helped to recognise how lonely anger can make people and how this could be avoided by taking a hold on himself, as he had shown that he could? Could one work out a strategy that encouraged him to work at self-control and at accepting responsibility for his behaviour, by frequent feedback on small and partial successes, while his unacceptable behaviour was firmly controlled? This would be to set him limits, while also protecting and building on what was 'good' in him, thereby giving him hope about himself by putting him in touch with the more mature parts of his self?

When the teachers were looking at John's behaviour in that light it was also possible to ask them to look at the choice that we ourselves have in the ways in which we look at others, especially those who defy us. We considered that such choice may have something to do with our own blind spots and that we might deal with these by trying to recall how our own powerful aggressions in childhood had been brought under control: we may then find remnants of our past experience of control in the temptation to respond aggressively now to pupils' provocations.

What I was suggesting was that, if we can learn that much about ourselves, it may be possible to deal with these remnants and prevent them from interfering with our professional skills, thus becoming more effective in teaching children whose desperation is expressed in aggressive behaviour, and that anger uncomplicated by such childhood residues will be of a different quality and more likely to produce the desired result than if it arises from our own insecurity, which we hate to be exposed.

Relieved that anger in the classroom need not be seen as unprofessional and totally condemnable and that some anger could be accepted as well placed and educative, the teachers then started to examine what opportunities one might create in the curriculum for helping young people such as John to understand and to handle angry feelings and the range of emotions that they are trying to come to grips with and to develop capacities for enriching relationships. They found that the whole range of subjects which they taught between them (social studies, English, art, mathematics, science, PE, French, 'child care and personality', commerce and remedial education) would lend itself, in content or method of approach, to such possibility (as we shall examine in Chapter 5).

All the members took an active, thoughtful part in these explorations, relating them to John and to the many others with such problems, but only a few of his teachers belonged to the group, which was concerned about those who had not taken part in the discussion. It was suggested that 'daughter groups' should be formed with his other teachers to enable them to confer systematically about appropriate strategies and about any further needs which emerged.

However, John reached a new crisis before this could be implemented, and his tutor (who had presented his case) pleaded with his seniors for John to be given another chance. Without further discussion with all those concerned in what this implied, the plea led to John's sudden promotion by two sets in mathematics as a sign of goodwill and to show confidence that he could do better. Unfortunately this involved a complete change of teachers; he lost not only those with whom he had had the worst confrontations but also those whom he had liked and those who had learned to understand him better and had begun to expect him to respond differently. The 'new chance' may have looked to him like rejection by those that he had taken to, so that the intended encouragement turned into loss for him. There had been no time for discussion with the new teachers of how the transition might best be handled and of the fears and hopes involved. Some of these teachers had seen his promotion as rewarding bad behaviour, so that his old reputation and the expectations attached to it preceded him. These expectations of trouble then fulfilled themselves, John's behaviour got worse, and his father was advised to move him to another school.

This was a painful lesson for the group but, although John was now beyond the reach of these teachers' better understanding, later cases had the benefit of it where lack of communication between staff might allow institutional processes to take the wrong course.

In all their following case discussions, and with cases not discussed, it became a matter of course to think of opportunities also in the curriculum which could help the teachers to combine their educational and enabling functions. They had found it useful to share and discuss their different reactions and ways of handling a provocative pupil and how to deflect his aggression instead of 'fixing' it with that 'fatal seriousness' (Erikson 1980) with which adults frequently respond to adolescents' experimental stances.

Dipak

This benefited Dipak, a Year 10 Indian boy, who was the next case presented. A shudder went through the group when his name was mentioned. Teachers had come to reject him for the 'creepy manner' with which he 'pestered' them with whining complaints and requests for special permission to come late, to leave early or not to attend games. By these means he hoped to avoid the other boys, whose bullying he attracted. With no friends in or out of school, he constantly sought help, mainly from women teachers – the men teachers, he said, frightened him. The women felt drained by his continuous waylaying and tried to cut him short when they could not fend him off or avoid him altogether; they could not bear his irritating manner.

He was, however, hardworking, especially in his mathematics set and quite imaginative in social studies. His work looked beautiful but was academically of a very poor quality and quite out of line with his grandiose ideas about his future; mad on aeroplanes, he wanted to become a pilot, from which his teachers tried in vain to dissuade him because of his poor work.

The teachers had little knowledge about his family, as his father spoke no English and his mother was living in India.

Teachers had tried to sympathise with him in the past but categorically refused to do so any longer; bullying had been dealt with, at senior level, as a racial issue, which the teachers did not think it was, since they felt that Dipak created his own problems. What had now lost him the teachers' sympathies was that 'he lied to us about a holiday in India' when he had simply played truant.

The partly nervous, partly hostile rejection of the boy in the group seemed total. They were unwilling to look for any positive features from which to start their exploration and demanded solutions from me, as definite as those which Dipak seemed to want from his teachers. I offered them none and they felt left in the lurch – as one could suppose that Dipak felt.

As the lie about the holiday in India appeared to constitute the point at which Dipak lost all sympathy, it seemed appropriate to deflect the discussion from

Dipak to feelings which people have when lied to. These ranged from anger at being thought stupid enough to fall for it, to outrage at the violation of deeply felt morals; but, I asked, were these always the intentions behind lies? Although people who lied did often want to get away with things, was lying not also frequently a defence against emotional difficulties or even a build-up of fantasies to bridge a seemingly unbridgeable ('unthinkable') gap between wish and reality? What if this particular lie, from a lonely boy, were such a fantasy, coupled perhaps with an illusion that fantasies can make the wish come true? What was this fantasy about, if not being where his mother was? Might there be some link between the missing, longed-for mother and his constant attempts to get help from the women teachers?

As the group followed this train of thought, they spoke again of his obsession with aeroplanes and the pilot fantasy now fitting into this picture. They accepted that terms such as 'liar' were better discarded as unhelpful labels which interfered with attempts at understanding people.

By eliminating the lie as a justification for rejection, the group could now focus on the boy's likely feelings and how the world must look to him; frightened of others in and outside school, he hoped that women teachers at least would understand and yet was unable to make them listen or relate to him, and he set about this in the most unsuitable way, possibly for want of any better experience at home in how to forge relationships.

It so happened that in earlier meetings there had been several references to the frustration that the teachers themselves felt when they were not listened to by their superiors. They had also felt let down by me when I did not give them the solutions that they demanded. I was therefore able to link this part of Dipak's experience with their own; not to be listened to by authority, whose job it should be to listen, was clearly very upsetting to most people. If, as they had said, Dipak was creating his own problems by the way in which he approached people, did that not happen to most of us? When we expect not to be listened to, do we express ourselves less well, appear to be demanding and thus help to create or reinforce the failure in communication? Had they not, for instance, allowed their seniors to treat Dipak's situation as one of racial bullying, although they themselves had thought there was more to it, so that impairment of his personal relationships, due to other factors, remained untackled?

With John's case in mind, the group then suggested that Dipak needed tutorial arrangements in addition to the existing academic ones, that he needed a focal point in the institution and that – in the light of his personal situation, and considering the kind of teachers that he was seeking out – there should be a woman tutor able to adapt her professional skills to his special needs, both to shelter and to stretch him. There were, after all, points in his work on which one could build, so that he could begin to feel a bit more accepted and thereby perhaps he could learn to accept himself more. Could such a tutor not also try to develop in him some social skills, help him to understand the reactions of others and see to it that, in class, group work was designed in such a way that he could practise such skills, especially if it involved those of his interests (e.g. aeroplanes) which others would be able to share?

Miss F, who made these suggestions, obviously saw how this could be initiated, and the group felt that, if she were to be Dipak's tutor, she would need his other teachers to fall in with her strategies. There would clearly be no easy way to achieve all this, considering what strong prejudice there now was against the boy; their own jittery reaction in the group, the derision and shudders with which they had earlier corroborated and extended details of the description had perhaps shown something of the social unconscious in relation to the features that they saw in him. They had at first, by their insistent demand for an immediate solution, hardly allowed me to help them to explore his case, which had made me feel momentarily as useless as the boy made them feel!

We could now understand that Dipak had multiple difficulties: his mother's permanent absence; a home and school with a great gulf between their cultures; perhaps a general rejection by the community. I reminded them of their own negative incapability earlier in the discussion and their irritable demands for quick solutions in a manner which implied that none could be found. (I had referred to Keats (letter, 21 December 1817) who referred to negative capability as 'when a man is capable of being in uncertainties, mysteries, doubts, without any irritable reaching after fact and reason...') More aware of their reactions to the boy's difficulties, they could now see these reactions as no longer totally alien to their own experience. They had seen for themselves how selective one's perceptions can be and how one tends to note behaviour which confirms one's constructs and to ignore or barely to notice behaviour which contradicts such constructs but which might, if observed, transform rejection into acceptance and help to repair damaged relationships. Aware of how they themselves were reproaching their superiors for behaving towards them as they behaved towards a pupil, they were able to appreciate that they were, on the one hand, adding to his hopelessness and, on the other, increasing their own frustration within the hierarchy.

Somewhat bemused by these turns in their preconceptions, the teachers decided to try Miss F's suggestions. She later reported that Dipak was responding to her approach and was beginning to be less tense with some other boys at least.

While examining Dipak's situation, we had also looked at the feelings which 'pupils whom one cannot teach' can generate and considered how these can lead to irritable demands on others – on pupils, on colleagues in the institutional hierarchy and, in this case, also on the outside consultant. These demands are often made in a way which can make those to whom they are addressed feel useless or hostile. We had thus taken John's case further by looking more closely at relations and communications in the institution itself and at the quality of the members' own negotiating skills when things were going wrong between teachers and pupils, between the pupils themselves or between colleagues. These are of course the issues emphasised by those who consult on individual problems within a 'systems approach', aware of the need to understand the interconnections between group functioning and the difficulties of individual members.

The group had met me weekly for two terms. Like some other groups, they then continued to meet on their own as a staff support group, inviting any other colleague to explore with them difficulties experienced with particular pupils, along the lines of the consultancy group. Two terms after its termination, interest was still growing among the rest of the staff, so that the formation of a second school group was being considered. Two years later, members of the original group still came to the intermittent follow-up meetings arranged for their area in one of their feeder schools.

Preparing the ground for additional professional help

Let us, lastly, look at discussion of the kind of case where more specialised help is needed but where the school tries to 'battle on' or where permission for referral is withheld – often this refusal to grant permission for referral becomes more determined, the more the school tries to put its case, thereby possibly exacerbating a parent's 'need to prove that she [is] right and "they" [are] wrong' (Dowling 1994).

Len

Mrs G, a teacher in another school-based group, had been valiantly trying to cope with Len, five and a half years old, and with the forceful grandmother who had brought him up, allowed his unmarried, tongue-tied mother no say in his upbringing and blamed the school for all his problems as listed by Mrs G. These were that Len was quite unable to concentrate, to coordinate his movements or even to use a pencil or to enjoy any activity, such as painting or sand play, which could improve his coordination. Never quiet or sitting still, he disturbed everybody very aggressively; he had not been taught how to eat without making a mess or when to go to the toilet, and so his food was everywhere and he smeared himself with excrement. He did, however, like doing sums and jigsaws, and Mrs G had always hoped that because of his brightness he would grow out of his difficulties, but this had not happened.

Discussing his symptoms, the group was helped to examine the probable confusions in this child's mind. His mother seemed too weak to claim him as hers, so that both she and the boy were treated as the grandmother's children. The daughter counted for nothing, and the grandson was always defended. Whatever he did was right in the grandmother's eyes; the child apparently ruled the household, and she placed the blame for his behaviour at school firmly in the school's court.

The situation seemed to be full of dissociations, and Len's needs too great for the school to meet without outside help, which the school now decided to ask for. In the meantime, the teacher's strategy of praise (which Len liked) and firmness (which he did not) could perhaps be combined, with both him and his grandmother. The group explored how this approach might be pursued with both, and especially with the grandmother, who was likely to resist the suggestion of child guidance help and would need the school's support (in spite of what they felt about her accusations!) to agree to take Len to the clinic – and to accept its advice.

The group returned to Len's case twice later that term. The grandmother's reaction against the idea of outside help had been even worse than expected; pounding her fist, she told the teacher and the head teacher that her own daughter had been 'messed about by the child guidance people' when she was small and that she would not 'let them now get hold of Len' – especially since her daughter was pregnant again and wanted to leave the home with Len to marry the baby's father.

The school, although unprepared for this flood of revelations, could now appreciate the grandmother's fears somewhat better. Further discussion enabled the teachers to be as supportive as possible, openly to appreciate her love for and attachment to Len and eventually to persuade her to take Len to the clinic. The grandmother warned them, however, that she would not 'open her mouth' there.

With these warnings, the group was encouraged to consider the grandmother's apparent fears and memories and was reminded of the many referrals for child guidance which do not survive the first appointment because of such fears and parents' reactions to being asked questions. This helped the school to prepare the clinic for this three-generation situation and the grandmother's anxieties. At the same time, the school endeavoured to give her consistent support as she continued her visits to the clinic, which Len then attended regularly. There his symptoms – some of which the teacher had not mentioned – were confirmed as signs of a severely distressed child, whom the school had seen as mainly a behaviour problem for them to cope with.

The school was enabled to give consistent support to the grandmother, whom they had formerly disliked for her hostility and her failure to appreciate their very real efforts to help Len. This helped him to receive and respond to the support which he needed. Four months later, Mrs G reported that the grandmother had now, in her own way, become one of the school's most ardent supporters, turning up at every parents' meeting. Len was beginning to be less messy, and his grandmother was delighted that the clinic had called him 'intelligent'. However, she still rejected the clinic's advice to place him in a special day school, although she was willing to have a look at one. She also accepted that Len's mother wanted to leave home and start life with a husband and both Len and the new baby. This was to be arranged without interrupting Len's school life and his bonds with his grandmother.

This case discussion had served to overcome the initial hostility between home and school and their mutual blame for the child's difficulties, and had enabled the school to give sensitive support to the key parent figure. When the teachers could see the grandmother as a frightened woman and her anger at Len's teachers as part of her anxieties, they could also cease rejecting her unfair accusations and appreciate her desperate need to prove that she was doing her best for Len. The grandmother in her turn could then change her feelings for them, as both sides began to listen to each other. As Bowlby (1985) stresses, 'In all this work there is no outcome more to be hoped for than one in which the corrosion of mutual blame is banished and its place taken by mutual respect and goodwill. For it is only then that durable solutions can be expected.'

The exploration also illustrates how experienced, competent and caring teachers may yet be unaware of, or uncertain about, the significance of their observations. Not knowing which problems may be transitory and which indicate more deep-seated difficulties, the school had wished to shelter a bright child from the professional help he needed and thereby unwittingly colluded with the grandmother's own irrational wish to protect the child from the help that he could eventually be given. Once his need for it had been accepted, the school then also saw that they had to help to secure it, both by skilfully briefing the clinic about the grandmother's memories and fears regarding child guidance and by supporting the grandmother during a time which they were helped to recognise as extremely stressful to her. In this way the process of referral could be experienced positively by both sides, which workers engaged with both family and school (Lindsey 1985) stress as a crucial aspect of school consultation.

Hitherto somewhat ambivalent in their communication with the clinic, the school felt that that link, too, was now much improved, as they were learning to approach them more as partners rather than defensively deferring to them as superior experts.

Summary

As we have seen, in none of these case discussions was there any attempt at issuing tips for teachers, or at telling others how to do their job and showing criticism of their methods. Instead, each case was jointly explored, with consultative guidance towards asking oneself the kinds of questions which might lead to better understanding of a child's exceptional needs and which might enable teachers to adapt their approach to the children in the course of their daily encounters. This took account of the teaching needs for immediate support as well as of their need for information which would highlight issues and evoke the skills necessary to put insights and principles into practice beyond the immediate difficulty. The solutions which they attempted were their own and arose from their active involvement in the joint exploration of workable alternatives.

The questions regarding the children were concerned with:

- their actual behaviour and the responses that it generated: particular incidents, their antecedents and consequences as they involved the child in relation to others;
- whether these suggested anything about how the child saw himself and others in relation to him;
- whether there were attitudes ('I'm no good', 'everybody is against me', 'it's their fault' or 'I can only get attention if...') which could be understood in the context of what was known about his circumstances;
- whether these suggested anything about unmet needs and the new learning experiences which might help to meet them and which the teacher might be able to provide consistently over a stretch of time.

Questions about adapting their approach to the needs identified involved the teachers in considering curriculum content and learning activities, ways of getting in touch with the pupil without intrusion and mistiming – crucial at adolescence but important at any age – so that he would not feel constantly observed or 'understood' at the wrong moment. These included:

- knowing when and how to convey recognition of the pupil's probable feelings about an incident, while setting him the limits that he might need;
- confronting the pupil constructively with his difficulty by building on his strengths, encouraging confidence and helping him to feel better about himself so that he can also see what is good in others;
- extending these experiences into the pupil's contacts with others at school and at home.

In this way, insight and skills were linked with the situation which had been presented as difficult, stressful and time consuming. What teachers found was that with unobtrusive interventions such as these they not only managed to to create a better learning environment for the children discussed as well as for the whole class. It also added to their own feelings of competence and of professional satisfaction. In order to keep the insight and skills elicited linked with the situation which had been presented for discussion, attention to essential focus points – agreed at the outset to be of likely importance – ensured a process of non-directively guided skilled sharing of experience between fellow professionals of equal but distinct expertise. We now have to turn in detail to these focus points, and to the different ways in which consultants may invite attention to them.

PART II

Continuing Professional Development: A Framework

Chapter 4

The Meetings: Conceptual Bases and Focus Points

Conceptual bases

While the consultative approach to collaborative staff development exemplified in the previous chapter is largely based on psychodynamic thinking, the examples also demonstrate the benefits of a flexible combination of complementary insights derived from interactional systems perspectives (Osborne 1994, Cooper *et al.* 1994) as well as behavioural ones (Berger 1979). This is in contrast with those who pigeon-hole single practices as whole answers to the complexities of a teacher's professional task, rejecting those which they perceive as belonging to – usually stereotyped – 'rival' schools.

It is the psychodynamic view that patterns of significant earlier experiences affect later ones, which can establish expectations and assumptions about later relationships and tasks to be met. The support then offered rests on the assumption that such expectations and responses can be superseded by new and specially structured learning experiences (see for instance Teresa's case (pp. 24–27). It is not seen as necessary for teachers to delve into a child's past to understand his present responses, since the responses themselves can tell us something about how a pupil sees himself and what he feels about others in relation to him. It is believed that pupils can be helped to cope with current problems that impede their learning, to the extent to which their feelings and anxieties are understood and such understanding is conveyed to them. As the examples show, teachers may not be able to 'solve' home problems but can do much to alleviate them if they recognise that they exist and attune their teaching accordingly.

Behavioural and psychodynamic approaches may, however, still be presented as opposites, and cognitive and affective curricular models as either/or approaches. As we saw in the consultation groups, however, teachers seemed to see no contradiction in focusing on here-and-now behaviour dynamics as well as considering such intangibles as present and past relationships and experiences. The aim was always to extend learning experience beyond the probable influences of past response patterns, to provide opportunities to experience new situations and to learn alternative ways of interacting. This implied that teachers had to be able to learn *from* the child. They helped the child to understand himself and his reactions without invading his privacy, as we saw for instance with Jeanie (pp. 38–41) and Tony (pp. 19–24). They used both psychodynamic and behaviour-oriented premises that, on the one hand, problematic behaviour (unless biophysically determined) expresses something for the child, arising from unmet needs and expectations rooted in the past and that, on the other hand, something in the present situation coincides with these expectations and helps to activate or maintain the difficulty. By establishing new learning experiences within a consistently constructive educational relationship, teachers could more fully realise the 'therapeutic' elements in educational procedures. This way of creating a better learning environment for the children was not only well within a teacher's scope but, as has been argued (Elliott 1982), is also clearly within the educational mandate. In contrast, where behavioural techniques remain purely manipulative, they may, unless expertly applied, produce short-lived changes specific to the situation, lead to mere conformism in the child or to repetitive and arid teaching and may lack the cognitive element required for a legitimate part of the educational process.

Focus points

Whatever a school's work setting, the rationale of the sessions described in Part I was, as we saw, to build on the teachers' experience and on their knowledge of the learning process, of child development and of human behaviour, while perceiving such knowledge as capable of supplementation by outside professionals or specially appointed members of staff with additional experience or special understanding of exceptional needs. As was shown, they need not themselves have met the child discussed or, if on the staff, may not know him as well as the teacher who presents his case. The process of joint exploration – whether with individual or groups of colleagues – with such a qualified colleague is utilised to enable teachers to redirect their perceptions and to answer for themselves the questions raised in the exploration rather than having them answered for them. Through examining the underlying issues in this way, they are more likely to see what may be wrong in the situation for a child and how they might make better use of their own skills and educational means to improve that situation and to help the child to cope, as they realise more fully the therapeutic potential that lies in any teacher's educational repertoire. They may then see how much more they can do as teachers faced with the individual needs of the whole range of children. They may come to realise that 'the challenge of "problem behaviour" can in fact become an opportunity for us as teachers to use our skills and professional judgement creatively...which may improve learning opportunities for all' (Mongon and Hart 1989).

In each session, with the focus on a specific child, knowledge and skills were shared which might help the teacher to understand and deal with that case better and the whole group with similar ones. *Knowledge* which would help to restore *objectivity* about the situation and *skills* which would heighten the teacher's *confidence* with regard to the task were shared, so that the teachers were able to muster their resources and to use them more effectively in support of the child's progress.

Knowledge was shared with regard to:

(a) the child, concerning how emotional, behaviour and learning difficulties develop (disturbance-producing experiences);
(b) the whole classroom group in relation to the child – as part of the dynamics of groups with regard to individual differences (disturbing behaviour may have a function for the group who could instead be helped to support his learning);
(c) managing the teacher–pupil interaction in the face of needs as gauged;
(d) the therapeutic potential in the day-to-day curriculum.

The skills which were shared related to:

(a) gauging the needs of a specific case from the behaviour displayed;
(b) making special bridging efforts to reach the child's 'teachable self';
(c) providing a consistent setting of new learning experiences likely to meet the needs gauged;
(d) involving, if possible, the child's parents and, if necessary, colleagues (fellow-teachers and members of other professions) as genuine partners.

Consistent attention to the issues underlying the specific case ensured that the whole group remained involved regardless of whether or not they knew the child discussed at any one session, and this helped the development of problem-solving skills for use in other cases. We must now see what this involved in detail.

Sharing knowledge

As we have seen, the consultant offers information as required for the understanding of the case under discussion beyond the behaviour displayed, to assist the discovery of ways of appropriate management. Its relevance must be clear, and it must be offered in a way which does not suggest that the consultant sees himself as sole expert and which will not further undermine the teacher's confidence, already likely to be dented by the difficulty of the case.

Secondly, it is clearly crucial – whether the consultant is a specially trained member of staff or an expert from outside – that the teachers are respected as autonomous professionals; thus the sharing of knowledge must reflect the consultancy principle of joint exploration between partners who contribute their equal but different expertise. The consultant's contribution is one among others. He helps to highlight the issues, balancing his input with joint exploration and heightening the teacher's sense of autonomy by encouraging them to draw on their latent resources and enabling them to approach their task with fresh understanding and confidence. This is at the same time an example of how the teacher might approach the pupil.

The consultant thus builds on the teacher's own professional knowledge which as a special needs or pastoral colleague he shares and which as an outside consultant he needs to make clear that he appreciates. Some of this may have become dated, outdated or inadequate; some of it may have become cliché-ridden and thereby arid, such as the 'self-fulfilling prophecy' or pseudo-explanations such as the 'broken home' and the 'one-parent family'.

As we saw in the case discussions, the information needed related to three main areas: the child 'out there', with his experiences which governed his reaction to situations; the child and his group of co-learners; the teacher in interaction with them.

(i) About the child

The child 'out there' may disappoint or affront teachers by rebuffing their best-intentioned efforts to help him to learn; the child may perplex them by going out of his way to make himself disliked; the child may make them feel useless because he won't try and is convinced that he cannot do what they require, as happens with so many discouraged children even when 'praised' (see Hanko 1994). In these and other ways the child invites and habitually receives the rejecting or despairing response which confirms his own expectations. This is in accordance with what is known about those 'aspects of perceptual distortion, inappropriate emotion and manipulative action (which tend to transform the present person and the present situation into the image and likeness of an earlier person and a past situation' (Irvine 1979)). As teachers deepen their understanding of such patterns, they find it increasingly possible to resist such attempts, to break out of the vicious circle in which they have been trapped and to help the child to find more fruitful ways of relating and to tackle his work with more hope.

The child's behaviour becomes understandable through applying information on how behaviour patterns are learned and how self-concepts are shaped to what is known of his circumstances and history. The group can then consider what approaches teachers can use to enable a child to establish different relationships with teachers and classmates, which can help to supersede his erroneous ideas about himself as hopeless, unacceptable and unworthy or about others as hostile, rejecting and indifferent.

Teachers found it useful to consider how children may try to deal with family anxieties in school, how they may be differently affected at different stages of development by what precedes and follows the break-up of a home, how siblings from seemingly intact families can confront their teachers with puzzling behaviour differences – which affect their learning – according to the different family roles imposed on them, how bereaved parents may hinder a child from expressing his own grief, how an abandoned parent may try to discredit the one who has left, unaware of the hazards for a child not allowed to think well of both his parents, and how this too may affect him at school.

As the underlying issues became clearer, no decisions were made for the teachers by providing clinical diagnoses or advice on treatment, nor was it suggested that they should tackle complex family relationships or strive to obtain such intimate knowledge beyond what parents willingly divulge. The teachers, on their own account, became more attentive to the clues available by discussing the implications of the issues, and this also helped them to respond more appropriately to the children's transient or long-term needs. We have seen how teachers learned to pay more attention to the situation in which a child began to behave in problematic ways and to his response to the measures taken to 'correct' this, and what these may represent to him. By viewing behaviour symptoms as part of a pattern of possible anxieties and defences against them, symptoms began to indicate the probable nature of the difficulty and of the kinds of learning experiences which might help a child to cope more effectively, in mutually satisfying and less crippling relationships.

(ii) About the classroom group

The child's group of co-learners, however, may not wish him to change – a frequent cause of frustration for teachers, when their sensitive handling of an individual child is brought to nothing by the reactions of the group, which may oppose his improvement. Undercurrents in the classroom, if merely controlled from the top or if left to themselves, can, as every teacher knows, block his every effort with one child whose peers may not 'allow' him to transcend his group role of troublemaker, victim, clown or scapegoat. One can then examine how the learning experiences which teachers may design for an individual pupil need to take into account the whole class for the child's sake as much as for the personal and social education of the others; this is as important as helping any particular child to see others in a new light. The pressures which operate in classroom groups, however, are frequently regarded by teachers as being 'in the nature of things', which they think they can do little to change other than by suppressing their worst features.

Teachers therefore found it useful to examine how groups, because of tensions in the group as a whole, can make use of particular individuals to express the group's needs and to understand the collusive roles played by other children in reinforcing individual behaviour difficulties. Having a class in hysterics at his deliberate antics may represent success for the class clown, staving off his fear that he might otherwise arouse their derision. Autobiographical accounts testify how behind children's many other 'nasty manoeuvres...[may lie] the hidden fear that [they themselves] might any moment fall from favour and become the object of contempt' (Clive James 1980). An understanding of group theory has helped teachers to see that the class clown may also be expressing something on behalf of the group and that other group roles may be similarly assigned – the rebel, the provocateur, the disrupter, the scapegoat and similar victims, the dunce, the swot and the conciliator. Each role expresses needs or desires for the other members of the group and is carried by the one for whom they are most urgent or least controllable, who is thus singled out to play the role and to suffer the restrictions that it can impose on his development as a whole person. As we saw in Don's and Martin's case (pp. 27–9 and 29–30), if a child is then helped to overcome such role restriction – a restriction with which Mrs B found she had colluded – or, if the bearer of such a role is absent or leaves, it may come to be adopted by another pupil. Most teachers have found this when rash enough to feel relief at the absence of a harassing child.

Better understanding of group processes and of the teacher's part in those processes can help them to consider what a classroom group may see as its purposes. Whether the purpose is cooperation with a teacher whom they perceive to be on their side, or rejection of another who appears to reject them, the group will collude with those of its members willing to express those wishes. Alerting teachers to these possibilities has enabled them to try out alternative methods of group management, to avoid collusion with a group's irrational needs, and instead activate the group's potential in support of each child's learning.

At the same time, information about the possible links between the needs of individuals and the dynamics of groups has helped teachers not to feel personally hurt, affronted, disappointed or surprised at unexpected undercurrents in overtly cooperative groups or individuals and to realise the potential for cooperation in those who are overtly hostile. It has helped them to steer these undercurrents towards more constructive support, even for the group's most vulnerable members.

To achieve this, teachers must know and remember how to foster the unifying forces in groups – feelings of belonging, self-esteem, constructive purpose, security in the absence of threat – and to reduce divisive tensions, such as rivalrous dependence on the teacher or on powerful group members, which may activate resentments and fears. Teachers can then see for themselves how their ways of managing a class, as well as ordinary curriculum content, can provide learning experiences (as we shall examine in detail in Chapter 5) to further the children's understanding of themselves and the world around them and to apply this in their relationships with each other.

If teachers can consider, in specific cases, that reparative forces may be latent in overtly opposed groups and individuals, they can also examine whether the climate of their institution influences their own readiness to work with or to oppose such forces as they exercise their authority. They can learn from such examples as Jimmy Boyle's (1977) ('Scotland's most violent man') account of his schooldays, when he felt, at ten years old, that the teachers who punished his violence so severely did not really want him to be less so, or as the 'relevant incident' used to highlight Dave's (pp. 35–8) and other cases.

These remind teachers of the choice which they may forget that they have – either to ignore this reparative potential and to leave it untapped, so that even the offenders remain unaware of it, or to learn to find and uncover it and to become able to 'confirm' the group and the pupil accordingly.

(iii) About the teacher–pupil interaction

Teachers can then see that the way in which we respond to children's needs and difficulties depends not only on our knowledge about children and the groups in which they move but also on how well we understand ourselves and our reactions to the range of special needs, especially if displayed in disturbing or abnormal behaviour. It is well known that, although we may be trained as professionals, we may continue to respond to the many difficulties that we encounter, not as professionals, but with our 'untutored selves' (Kahn and Wright 1980). Not to do so requires self-awareness and, for teachers, an understanding of the personal aspects which may influence relationships between teachers and learners. The case discussions illustrated two main features of the learning process in consultancy support groups: that members should develop sufficient understanding of what is 'out there' in the object of the investigation and that they should note and deal for themselves with what assumes personal significance for them. As has already been stressed and demonstrated (e.g. in Dave's case discussion (pp. 35–8)), the absence of a mandate for taking up personal references in consultancy – which is not psychotherapy – requires that such self-understanding should be furthered only through reference to what is universal in such relationships, and without reference to individuals.

We saw in John's case (pp. 41–4) how this may be done. There, the group examined how a pupil's bad feelings about himself may be aggressively projected onto 'convenient' teachers. It briefly considered the links between the way in which our own aggressions had been handled when we were children and the demands that we may later make on others and thus influence how convenient a target we become for their aggression. If this is understood, teachers become aware of how a whole range of anxieties relate to what we feel about success, failure and inadequacy and to the demands that we make on ourselves and others. This can help teachers to handle and even to forestall those battles with pupils in which both sides feel persecuted and picked on by the other and in which the defensive provocations of one side become 'evidence' of the other's badness. When this was put as generally valid – i.e. not concerning just one teacher – teachers themselves saw how one may be tempted to 'deal with' a pupil so as to stop his expressing and challenging one's own unacknowledged doubts about one's competence. They could also see that acceptance of doubts and difficulties, far from reflecting negatively on their competence, could in fact add to it and that, if they understood the possibility of such mutual 'projective identifications', they found it easier to survive their impact. By not retaliating, they could help a pupil with his feelings, gently reflecting them back to the pupil and acknowledging that he will have reasons for them, and could help him to see that, even if one has such reasons, one does not have to act them out on others. We saw how this had helped, for instance, Tony (pp. 19–24) and Vic (pp. 32–5).

To apply insights such as these requires teachers to try to understand what they themselves are made to feel by their pupils and then to use this self-understanding to gain access to the pupil's related problems, to his experience and eventually to his 'teachable self'. What Oakeshott (1973) called discovering the pupil's 'conflict-free areas' needs to be preceded by widening one's own. Both are aided in the consultancy process, without having to bring any teacher's actual feelings into the discussion.

As we have seen, teachers enjoy the full involvement in the sharing of knowledge which arises if the consultant maintains a balance between contributing his expertise and eliciting theirs. In different sessions, this balance may be tilted one way or the other, as we saw in the case study sequences. The consultant can restore the balance if he too asks for help and clarification and admits that he lacks the knowledge which others in the group possess – such as their knowledge of the children that he may not know or, in the case of an outside consultant, matters of institutional organisation which he has not himself experienced. Caplan (1970) finds that the consultant's expertise is best offered by 'asking answerable questions' to generate insight, without undermining the group members' confidence, which may have been damaged by their failure to solve the problem. If one includes oneself among those who might not at once have understood what was happening (for instance by suggesting that 'most children could react in this way when they misunderstand us as happened here, but we may not always notice it when we are in the midst of it'), one opens the door to more information about behaviour patterns as well as to alternative approaches to them. By acknowledging limitations the consultant makes it easier for others to do so. All the time, he acknowledges and works with the teachers' daily experience, from which he is, as specialist, sufficiently distant, however, to act as a more objective outsider whose questions can throw light on or reveal gaps in their awareness and their unexplored assumptions about teaching and learning. If the consultant shares his knowledge in this way, teachers are more likely to examine its validity and to test out its implications.

At the same time, offering information as part of a process of joint exploration and genuine questioning is a teaching technique in its own right and likely to be of special interest to teachers, which they may be willing to develop further in their own classrooms, alongside other techniques which they employ.

Restoring objectivity

When personal feelings have intruded into the work situation, a teacher may find it difficult to deal with a pupil objectively. As we saw in the case discussions, a teacher may show that he prefers or rejects a pupil on grounds of positive or negative identification with him. This will cloud the teacher's judgement and influence the way in which he uses his authority. The teacher may overreact or even abdicate in the face of actual or perceived challenges to his competence if he himself harbours doubts about it. Alternatively, he may take a subjective stance arising from deeply held convictions about life and learning, and may feel under pressure from superiors, from pupils' parentsm, or from what the public at large seems to demand of teachers.

The consultant will notice these problems only through what the teacher contributes to the discussion. He has to judge whether to use these contributions now or later, when any tension has passed and alternatives have become clearer. The consultant thus tries to gauge the 'space between the words': between what has been said and what seems to be implied and between what may be purposely concealed, which has to be respected as private, and what remains unsaid because the teacher may be unaware of features which, if brought into the open, might turn out to be untapped resources waiting to be used.

Different levels of communication and their significance in the consultancy setting have been discussed by others. Schein (1969), for instance, differentiates between four areas of the self:

(a) the 'open self' (or what we are prepared to reveal about ourselves);
(b) the 'concealed self' representing what is deliberately kept from others (this, as Caplan also emphasises, has to be respected as personal in the consultancy process);
(c) a 'blind area' of the self (the 'blind self'; our blind spots) which we conceal even from ourselves but which may be noticeable to others (for instance, the consultant and group may notice when a teacher seems to add to his problems with pupils without realising it);
(d) an 'unknown self', unknown to the person and to others (Schein considers this part of the self irrelevant for the purposes of consultation – surprisingly so, since this unknown self can be the area of hidden strengths, skills, potentialities and is capable of being tapped in the catalytic process of consultancy).

Contributions reflective of all four 'selves' are likely to be made in case discussions.

There appears to be no difficulty about the 'open self'. However, communication which is too intimate and personal may present problems to a consultancy group. A teacher may, for instance, describe a child's experience openly as 'identical' with his own childhood experience, as happened in the case of a pupil whose learning was presented as impeded by an over-demanding parent who set impossible standards. The consultant has to resist the temptation to explore this further and to continue to focus on the child in question and the search for a solution to his problem, without appearing to rebuff the teacher's personal remark. Such identification with the child (noticeable through comments such as 'I know what this child is going through; it happened to me') may also distort the teacher's perception since, if the child's situation becomes linked with his personal vulnerabilities, the teacher may project his own feelings and problems onto the child, and his activity on the child's behalf may be distorted. In the 'severe father' case, for instance, we learned from the teacher that he was unable to avoid speaking to the father in a rejecting, demanding tone of voice, which effectively prevented the father from accepting his suggestions. The teacher was helped to realise that, instead of fighting the father, he might be of more use to the boy by helping him to cope better with the father's demands, as possible signs of concern for his son's future. Changing his feelings about the father, the teacher then managed to help him to appreciate the very real efforts that his son was making, to discuss matters calmly with him, to acknowledge his concern and to help him to support the boy's gradual progress. Another teacher mentioned how irritating she found one of her girls, second in a family of three daughters ('like myself'), whose mother constantly compared her unfavourably with the two others when she spoke to the teacher, and the teacher herself responding to the girl as she said her own mother had done to her. The group explored how one might help the child to be less irritating and then to let the mother see the teacher's growing acceptance. This in turn seemed to make the teacher more relaxed about the girl to whose provocative negativism she could now respond calmly and constructively, managing what Irvine (1979) refers to as responding 'to the reality of the other person, with ability to perceive his qualities, and to feel and react appropriately', instead of colluding with the child's own tendency to distort her relationship with the teacher in accordance with her experience of a fault-finding mother. Conversely, in another group a teacher presented the difficulties which she had with an adolescent girl who, while getting on well with other teachers, singled her out as a convenient target for defying authority – while the teacher herself had been in constant battle with the new head teacher whose authority she resented. The group discussed, in general, feelings of defiance towards an authority figure and their impact, and whether one might find ways of eliciting and strengthening latent, more constructive, alternative feelings in such pupils, acknowledging but, in the process, also setting limits to the anger displayed. The teacher participated eventually in exploring how this might be done and thoughtfully commented on 'what an experience it is to be at the receiving end of such outbursts'.

Finding such workable solutions in itself tends to reduce the anxiety felt about a case, whether or not it is connected with the teacher's personal life. However, where personal remarks suggest such a link, it is possible briefly to acknowledge them with the respect which is owed to reflected past pain and to accept them as illuminating the situation under discussion, without entering further into them. The focus can then remain on the pupil and the manifest problem, preserving the consultant–teacher relationship as one of objective joint exploration. Throughout, however, the consultant has been communicating at various levels; he has heard the teacher's manifest message (as in these cases the boy's learning difficulty and the girl's irritating behaviour) and also noticed, without explicit acknowledgement, the latent message (about the children and the teacher's own 'harmful parent') which was tacitly attended to (by seeing the parents' behaviour as a symptom perhaps open to modification if they heard of their children's progress in a way which also accepted the parents).

As to our 'concealed' and 'blind' selves, it is perhaps the most seminal aspect of this form of support that private, or even unconscious experience which may be interfering with the professional task, is respected as private, while its possible significance for the work setting is not ignored. Teachers often bring into a presentation several themes, such as their feelings about the child, the parents and the role of mothers or fathers, or feelings about themselves in relation to the school. They may do this wittingly or unwittingly. Consciously or unconsciously, a teacher may agree with a parent's criticisms of the school and yet resent his or her raising them but not feel free to discuss this in the group. There may be unresolved ambivalence if the teacher himself has attracted some of the parent's dissatisfaction, deservedly or underservedly. In the exploration, one may be able to discuss in general terms the roots of dissatisfaction – one's own and that of others – and alternative ways of dealing with it, before looking at the particular parent's reasons as perhaps lying partly in the school and partly in himself. The school could then become a conveniently available target for the parent, the school having certain insufficiencies to which some parents may feel antipathy for personal reasons. It may be useful to consider alternative responses to other people's projections and perhaps to discuss parents' responses to our own insufficiencies and how we may attribute to them what we feel about our imperfections. Teachers tend to be staggered, relieved and stimulated by 'simple' suggestions that what others think about us may be seen as their problem, but our reaction to this is ours and may well affect their attitude. They are staggered because the relevance for most of those discussing a case is immediately appreciable; they are relieved because it is presented as universal, and stimulated to tackle what real grounds there may be in the complaints. This also helps to sensitise them to the anxieties underlying complaints which prove to be groundless, as was illustrated in Len's case (pp. 48–51).

All this appears to be well within the scope of a staff support group but, since objectivity, and not therapy, is the aim, any such discussion must remain relevant to the case under discussion and professional relationship involved. This enables the personal side, concealed or blind at first, to begin to inform professional action in aid of the child's learning. We shall see later to what extent the parents can be involved in similar ways.

Seeing their own privacy thus respected, teachers find that they can acknowledge the privacy of their pupils and can develop an ability to respond to their special emotional needs without violating this as part of the curriculum and school experience. Tony's case (pp. 19–24) showed how respect for this principle helped a child to share his distress with his teacher without talking about it and so to cope with it better. However, secrets 'kept dark' and yet obviously accepted in the group in general terms – such as the fact that problems occur regardless of length of career experience – may become openly admitted, respected, survived and found worth sharing objectively. Teachers found that secrecy about unavoidable failures had in fact added to the strain, further sapping their confidence, when failure accepted and jointly examined helped to restore it. It had been used to illuminate the task and not turned into a judgement of the person.

Partial successes are frequently discovered within perceived failure, and resources from the 'unknown self' may become manifest and usable for deliberate strategies. An advantage of the continuous support (of a length sufficient to permit follow-up discussions) is that teachers can become aware of changes in their perception and interpretations of a child's behaviour between the initial presentation of a case and follow-ups, and discussion can bring out new responses to a child's individual needs. It then becomes clearer how the use or non-use of our professional skills depends on what details we notice about a child, how we interpret them and how we may distort what we perceive and then narrow each new perception in accordance with past distortions. The hackneyed concept of the self-fulfilling prophecy comes to life through catching oneself in the act, when a child's behaviour is seen to change in response to changing perceptions and anticipations, as we saw in Dave's case (pp. 35–8). Teachers reported that their perception sometimes changed even on their way home from the meeting. On one occasion, a teacher found that her perception changed even as she was planning to present a difficult boy ('who had given nothing but trouble the whole year') to the meeting later that day and 'for the first time, strangely enough, he was all right to today', his behaviour changing in response before he was ever discussed at all!

It is clearly crucial that teachers should be aware of the role that we play in the processes of selective attention which influence our judgements and should recognise how these judgements affect their objects, how our feelings about pupils, influenced by such selective attention, are communicated to them in our reactions and how our lost objectivity may unwittingly collude with the pupil's own predispositions and lead to a re-enactment of his situation. Britton (1981) has analysed how trying to resist such unconscious collusion may go against the grain of a professional worker's own emotional inclinations. Hargreaves' (1972) application of Laing's concept of 'metaperspectives' to the classroom and the teacher–pupil relationship is relevant here, as it describes how both a pupil's and a teacher's perceptions, interpretations and reactions – all those 'projective efforts after meaning' – may lead them to ascribe the best or worst possible intentions to the other. Since Abercrombie's (1969) description of her teaching technique with medical students, there have been a number of attempts to achieve awareness of such issues through approaches to the curriculum. We shall return to this point when we look at the relevance of curriculum skills to meeting individual needs. What matters here is that in the consultancy process a potentially vicious spiral of self-confirming negative projections can be interrupted and that teachers may find themselves able to start its virtuous counterpart. They are then in a better position to do what Wall (1973) has stressed as uniquely within their scope; with objectivity restored, instead of accentuating further the difficulties which may have created the special needs, teachers capable of getting through to the children can then offer them a consistent set of new learning experiences in a genuinely re-educative process.

Sharing skills

As we have seen, the skills which this requires are, first of all, the ability to see beyond the behaviour displayed, to *gauge a child's needs* which the behaviour may mask. This involves unobtrusive observation, appraisal (of how, for instance, assertive behaviour may mask a low self-concept (Burns 1982)) and reappraisal as needs evolve. Secondly, *special bridging efforts* have to be made to reach the child's 'teachable self'. The teacher needs to be able to perceive and to build on what is good in a child, to listen and to share his experience without intruding, to express acceptance and to convey to the child unostentatiously that his words and acts are understood as signs of the child's anxiety. The child may be able to bear these anxieties because they are understood and they need then not interfere so much with his work and relations with classmates. His feelings are being made manageable through the opportunity of airing them with somebody seen as supportive. We saw how Tony's teacher (pp. 19–24) skilfully intervened in the child's crisis behaviour, offered him support while setting limits to the behaviour and helped him to start learning again. With these skills, she found the 'area which was free of conflict' and could meet 'the teachable part of the self' (Oakeshott 1973). This requires a third set of skills: *the setting of learning experiences and presentation of educational material* in such a way that these help to amend the limiting ideas that the child may have developed about himself in relation to others and to the tasks which he is set. This is done through encouragement strategies, the use of 'confirming skills' and of curriculum content and attention to classroom dynamics and to the special management of potential disturbance points in the educational system and educational institutions (such as first entrance, end-of-year changes, change of teachers, and changing and leaving school).

Teachers in the groups were almost invariably surprised at their underuse of quite basic techniques of encouragement and recognition which they said that they valued but which they 'forgot' to use with their most troublesome pupils – who, they admitted, needed them most. Gulliford (1971) touches on this paradox in his discussion of Redl's teaching techniques with 'children who hate' (Redl and Winemann 1957).

As I have tried to show, if teachers are to discover and develop their ability to respond to individual needs, there should be no prescription in staff support groups of what they ought to do. While the consultant helps them to focus on the underlying issues, he also helps them to see what skills they need to employ to ensure the learning experiences required by individual children. In one such case, as we saw, a teacher presented unresponsive, prickly ten-year-old Ivan (pp. 15–18), whom he 'could not teach anything' and who did not respond even to praise on the one occasion when he had unexpectedly produced some very imaginative writing about one of Kipling's *Just-so Stories*, which the teacher had read to the class. Praising him for it the next day, after he had had time to read the children's writings, the teacher found that Ivan was 'back in his shell'. When this case was discussed in the group, the content of the story – 'How the hedgehog got his prickles' – was found to be revealing; only then did the teacher himself recognise the therapeutic meaning which the story had for the child, which he had failed to see at the time. The teacher could then find a way of taking the class into the theme of protection and survival, showing respect and admiration for the hedgehog's way of defending himself against danger, as Ivan had done in his writing. Rather than having his work merely praised out of context, it could be accepted as part of the work of the class. Some of Ivan's needs were being understood at a deeper level, and one could begin to meet them in new learning experiences with his classmates.

Again it was the teacher who was left to decide how this might be attempted. As had been the case with Tony's teacher (pp. 19–24), he used his skills as a result of understanding better a specific incident (note in this context Redl's (1966) account of such therapeutic communication, particularly as emotional first aid) and then as part of the general interaction with pupils in their normal school activities. The teacher did not need to get closer to the child than either of them could bear, a point which has been stressed as crucial for the therapeutic use of educational skills (Caspari 1975).

Restoring confidence

Clearly, it helps to restore confidence if one can develop one's capabilities in this way. The teachers' confidence may have been sapped for various reasons. Some teachers could see how they had misinterpreted as personal challenges children's rejection of their teaching, and others how their own perfectionist views on what a teacher ought to achieve or is 'entitled' to expect from pupils had made them defensive and induced a sense of failure and incompetence when their expectations were disappointed. This had made it even more difficult to gain access to the children whom they found difficult.

The consultant ensures that the focus remains on the pupil and the manifest problem; yet, as was shown, he works at different levels of communication. While the consultant helps the group to deal with pupils' failures and successes, success and failure in general become a professional issue, indirectly helping members in the repair of their own loss of confidence and self-esteem. One finds that assisting teachers to help their pupils to cope with felt inadequacy and insufficiencies often means that teachers become more able to accept their own vulnerabilities and, by accepting them, to turn them into capabilities – without specific reference to any individual teacher. (We shall see in Chapter 6 how a similar situation arose between teachers and parents.)

Most teachers seemed, until then, to have regarded success and failure, their own and that of others, in purely subjective terms, as a reflection on the person. Only now, some said, could they look more dispassionately at their difficulties, to see what these could tell them about the task in hand. It is clearly important for teachers to be able to do this and to understand the educational significance of helping their pupils to experience success and failure as showing whether or not one is 'on the right track' (Bruner 1961), rather than seeing them as cause for reward and punishment emanating from an institutional hierarchy. Where the latter experience dominates, we may wish to demonstrate our successes and to hide our failures, with effects on our self-esteem, confidence and motivation – influencing whether we make decisions in obedience to authority or critically on moral grounds. The relevance for teachers of this issue was shown in Milgram's (1974) studies which suggested that what influenced whether people developed sufficient self-confidence to analyse the problems confronting them and to solve them appropriately, or whether they merely wanted to perform competently on authority's terms, had much to do with their past rewards for deference to authority figures. A school's authority pattern was seen by the researchers as one of the antecedent conditions which affect self-confidence and motivation to proceed with one's tasks in any other way than that of obedience (or irrational rebellion against authority), or to assist the development of a positive self-concept on the basis of which one becomes the arbiter of one's actions.

These are important considerations for any organisation which is concerned for the motivation of its members. They assume special significance for institutions whose aim is the education of self-regulating individuals capable of assessing their own positive potential. As is now increasingly recognised, unless teachers are themselves capable of such self-regulating assessment and in the process become more able to look for what is positive in their pupils, the way in which they are or are not acknowledged by colleagues and superiors continues to have an effect on how they acknowledge others and on what happens between them and their pupils. (The point that teachers should be capable of self-regulating assessment tends to be forgotten by those who suggest that teacher assessment could be tied to merit money links and/or observation in the classroom by superiors. This not only alters the performance in the process but also polarises those deemed to possess the required skills and those deemed not to.) Teachers found this an issue of absorbing interest as they examined specific pupils' interactions with them, assessing and improving their performance without being 'told' that they needed to do so.

Chapter 5

The Curriculum: Finding Opportunities to Attend to Children's Emotional and Social Realities in Support of their Learning

The examples given in Chapter 3 have shown how, regardless of a group's work setting, consideration of a specific case enabled the staff, across departments and hierarchies, to explore wider issues arising from it. The significance of seemingly baffling behaviour, the underlying needs that it may indicate, what responses might be appropriate and the need to understand one's own reaction to the needs expressed are examples of the issues which arose. We saw the considerable capital of latent skills and personal resources such explorations can tap in teachers and make available for use in the classroom. Teachers welcomed the chance of discovering and deciding for themselves how they might improve a pupil's situation. We saw how these processes developed and how their development in the core attenders of a staff support group (who chose to attend the group from first to last with a view to initiating other development groups, see Part III) benefited short-term members and newcomers who learned – from the questions which were being asked in the group – how to look for workable solutions. By extending their knowledge of the way in which situations and backgrounds can affect a specific child's learning, teachers were able to relax their hold on preconceived ideas about the child in question and their own ineffectiveness with him. The group helped them to look with fresh eyes at the situation, to see it also from the pupil's point of view, to respond more adequately to his needs, both through curricular interactions (their way of interacting with him and the rest of the class) and through increased awareness of the affective potential in curriculum content. We saw how teachers became more objective in 'attuning' their encouragement techniques (Hanko 1994) to their pupils' experiences and were more able to make demands on them in a way which made it possible for the pupils to meet these.

It has been of interest to teachers in mainstream schools how many of those with comparable experience in the special education field have long suggested to their colleagues in either sector that their teaching could be enriched if they learned from each other's curricular developments. Suggestions have covered the range of subjects and how these might be taught so as to be both intellectually challenging and personally significant, with pupils able to examine solutions to *actual* difficulties and conflict situations in the shape of *typical* ones which are part of the human condition they are learning to understand (Elliott 1982). Rutter's argument (see Chapter 3) about providing for children benevolent 'positive school experiences of both academic and non academic kinds' (1991) was not about sheltering them from the dilemmas of life but about helping them to become resilient in facing them.

The argument for the educative potential of attending to the emotional and social aspects of an academic curriculum is that learning to understand the human condition and the part which emotions play in people's lives, and learning to accept responsibility for one's relationships and behaviour in the face of obstacles and pressures, enhances that curriculum. Such an enhanced curriculum, important for all children, will, as we have seen, also be adaptable to the needs of pupils with emotional and behaviour problems who need to feel, even more than others, that their efforts to express their needs can be heard, recognised and satisfied within the school, through cooperation rather than conflict. Only such a curriculum, broad, balanced and adapted to their individual needs as well as to those of all others will ensure that 'excellence for all' (DfEE 1997a, b), which the government trusts teachers to achieve.

As we have seen, however, teachers do not always make full use of their educational resources, especially if sidetracked by some children's behaviour into surface behaviour management, mistaking this as a sufficient response. They do not always pay enough attention to those methods, activities and contents within the curriculum which would allow these children, too, to experience themselves as more successful academically, socially and personally and which would enable them to learn to understand and manage their feelings and to build up a concept of self-worth. The Elton Report (DES 1989) consequently recommended that schools should develop an 'affective curriculum' in response to children's emotional realities. Since then, the call for better understanding of children's feelings to meet their personal and social needs in support of their learning (National Curriculum Council 1989) has led to numerous suggestions for subject areas across the school curriculum.

We have seen how in the consultation groups such better understanding promoted attention to the therapeutic potential in the ordinary teaching programme, enabling teachers to get in touch with a child's 'teachable self' (Oakeshott 1973). Teachers became more alert to the opportunities in the general educational programme to design learning experiences which could help children to deal better with the problems in their lives (while respecting the problems as private), to feel better about themselves and to widen their understanding of themselves, their world and the possibilities and limitations of choice which are open to them.

An increasing number of practitioners (Clark *et al.* 1997, Hart 1996, Mongon and Hart 1989) have been discussing arrangements designed to strengthen this dimension of learning in the whole school, such as extending the expertise of the special needs and pastoral care staff to all their colleagues, to enable them to help children 'without always giving individual help' (Marland and Rogers 1997). Researchers and practitioners have stressed that to initiate such arrangements through systematic supportive discussions with groups of colleagues should be considered a proper part of a school's development plan (DfE 1994), with the assistance of staff from the educational and psychological services (DfEE 1997c). Working with colleagues in this way and for this purpose naturally asks for particular skills and understanding. (This is an issue to which we shall return in Part III). An awareness of the therapeutic potential in the whole curriculum range, beyond one's own subject expertise, will be one aspect of this, and a crucial qualification for such collaborative curriculum coordinators if they want to achieve credibility with their colleagues individually or in groups (Hanko 1989), and to focus attention on what it may be possible to achieve 'pastorally' within each discipline and its related learning activities.

The teachers in our groups, for instance, found an increasing number of ways of introducing into the curriculum accounts of the kinds of experiences which were of concern to the children. This enables children to speak of their own experience if they wish to but explores it in general terms as it is reflected in literature or other accounts used. This has of course been advocated as good educational practice for many years. Time-honoured pedagogical procedure, however, still tends to keep school subjects separate from those 'basic themes which give form to life and learning' (Bruner 1968), and this makes it harder to engage the children's personal knowledge, concerns and emotional energy constructively in their learning. Collaborative consultancy helped teachers to find ways of linking personal experience with curriculum content; in other words, of linking 'caring' with 'teaching' (Morris 1991) by presenting subjects in such a way that the children's life situations are unobtrusively included in the curriculum, at one remove and as part of the human condition which their education is to help them to understand. Teachers found that this can be done in spite of an examination-focused teaching schedule as it continues to be imposed on schools, and that such teaching need not – and must not – mean any lessening of conceptual rigour.

Pupils' concerns as an integral part of the curriculum: no lessening of conceptual rigour

The teachers agreed that such teaching can be both academically and personally inspiring. This was confirmed by a former student's recollection of her *history* teacher when he played them sections of Beethoven's ninth symphony as an introduction to the historical events of that time, and how this had stimulated both a lasting interest in history and an awareness of how *music* can touch people's lives. Teachers working with troubled children in special schools come to mind who, aware of how music affects learning and mood, play classical music during lesson time (now the subject of a research paper by Hallam and Katsarou, delivered at the 1998 meeting of the British Educational Research Association (McGill 1998)). The debates on Music and Politics (the subject of the 1998 BBC Promenade Lecture (Steiner 1998; see also Clements 1998), show other cross-curricular opportunities. The 'Politics of the Romantic Hero' (BBC 3, 1998) are now discussed as a response to industrialisation, the rise of mass culture and disillusionment with the results of the French Revolution, and can lead to examining modern protest lyrics. The visual arts and their place in society are an equally rich source for discussion, raising issues of freedom, democracy, censorship, authoritarian versus authoritative leadership.

Exploring issues like these can include all those methods that teachers have developed to make children aware of what *language* can do, both cognitively and affectively. They require teachers to be willing to listen to children finding a voice of their own in the toings and froings 'from curriculum to communication' (Barnes 1976, Davie and Galloway 1996, Davie *et al.* 1996, Hart 1996). The Warnock Committee considered language development to be even more crucial for children with exceptional needs than for those with fewer problems or subject to less stress. But all children need help to understand what they feel and to give words to it. These are learning experiences with language designed to encourage self-awareness and an understanding of responsibility in relationships.

Teachers in the consultancy groups found no difficulty in examining such possibilities both in general and with regard to specific cases (see Ivan, pp. 15–17). They explored how to create opportunities to help children to understand how people affect each other by their attitudes and behaviour. 'Soaps' like *EastEnders* were considered a goldmine with adolescents for examining how the characters contribute to their relationship difficulties by their attitudes, behaviour and all those negative communications of not listening, interrupting others, telling them what to do without understanding, in contrast to those that convey sensitivity to others in distress. This could be used to teach listening skills and *communicative competence*, developing an understanding of how language works, the feelings it can or may not be able to convey. Linked with textual analysis, this can include children discussing each others' finished work, saying what they felt about the way their work was marked, learning to mark that of their peers with a positive comment and constructive advice, feeling their own knowledge and experiences as worth talking about, as well as learning about asking questions that foster understanding versus those that close discussion, or are experienced as hurtful (Gold 1998). At the same time, awareness of regional and social variations in language use (the *EastEnders'* expression of 'getting sorted' has now entered the English language!) in different settings, of appropriateness and intelligibility, can help to teach tolerance and empathy.

In collaborative inter-school groups (see Chapter 3), teachers across the age range of school attendance can share their expertise in using *imaginative literature* for understanding life's concerns and challenges. Using such literature has always been good practice with primary school teachers who use make believe play, story materials that help children to make sense of their own situations and share this with others, stories which introduce children to the world's literature, or improvised drama alongside direct teaching methods (Peter 1995). This allows children to 'experiment' with their own problems in the disguise of fictional or real characters, to express feelings or anxieties liable to interfere with relationships and educational progress, methods of creating 'imaginary' worlds which illuminate the 'real' world which pupils are facing. What fascinates children across the world about 'the old implausible fairy tales are the emotional conflicts they express in a world where bad things can happen and that difficulties can be dealt with, conflicts can be resolved, that there is a dark side to life, to come to terms with, to master it' (Bettelheim 1985; see also Green 1996, Steel 1998).

The range of human feeling and experience which literature can open to children of all ages and attainments, how people through the ages tried to deal with matters of life and death, to cope with separation, tragedy and loss, reaches from ancient myths, legends, folk tales to modern tales for young children. Grove and Park (1996) in their *Odyssey Now* have made Homer's tale accessible in dramatised form to all children across the age and achievement range, while they learn about empathy with Oscar Wilde's The Happy Prince, or wonder with tales like 'the Giant who was Afraid' whether one can be brave and nervous at the same time' (Davies 1983). Stories about young animals and their growing independence while still needing an adult to protect them acknowledge implicitly, and at a safe third 'person' distance, the children's own relationship, and the feelings that are part of them. (As well as designing aspects of the *general* curriculum so as to arise from the children's own experience, teachers have also been able to help children to discover for themselves, at an unobtrusive *individual* level, what they may gain from books which deal with everyday and specific problems, adding such books to the school library. Some local libraries (e.g. Leicestershire) have established selections of 'help at hand' books, available to schools, which sensitively show how children grapple with experiences of fear, pain, hope and disappointments as they face the problems of adults' tensions and quarrels, family losses and realignments. It is, however, important to use such books incidentally and choose only stories which do not come too close to the child's actual situation, portray too idealised a picture of relationships, moralise or contrive solutions which cannot speak to the children's condition or which in other ways betray that they do not accept their problems as serious. An examination of the whole field of bibliotherapy in relation to children has been made by Crompton

(1980). (See also the Appendix to this book, for the list of books compiled by the staff of a children's hospital school (see Steel and Ofield 1998 in the Bibliography) and which may assist teachers compiling their own collection of books).

Teachers have been using real life diaries, letters, such as selected poems and anthologies by well known poets, from *The School Bag* (Heaney and Hughes, eds, 1997) or selected poems from Ted Hughes' *Birthday Letters* (1998). A group of pupils, wanting to help those suffering from famine in Ethopia, themselves wrote to famous people, invited them to name their favourite poem and to give reasons for their choice, then compiled the responses in an impressive *Lifelines* anthology (Macgonagle, ed., 1993). Children across the age-range of school attendance are stimulated into writing their own poems when studying those of popular children's poets like Causley, McGough or Rosen, who tackle serious issues, as well as those that can make us laugh. We heard of children's own moving poems, some of them about lasting pain of loss and coping with troubling experiences, others expressing seemingly light-hearted ambivalence, like the 11-year-old boy's 'I have a little brother, and never want another...'!

Children making up their own stories lead us into the field of *media studies* with their cross-curricular potential. We heard of stories like 'a day in the life of a penny' (daily household economics), 'a cell's experience of the human body' (stimulated by Professor Winston's 1998 television series on that topic) and of 'a diesel engine's trip across France' (science, geography, foreign languages). Computers and websites can become means of publishing their work, of communicating with the wider world and sharing it with that world. The Children's Express 'programme of learning through the process of journalism' (1998) involves children in activities such as interviewing other children about good and bad school experiences. Interviewing pupils whose school had been in the media spotlight opened their eyes to what the headlines did to them, how they had not recognised themselves as those skinheads depicted, and how the good things about them, such as their hard work for their exams, were omitted; the vilification of the Ridings School boy, with no mention of having just lost a brother in a car accident, are all lessons that will help children not only to become aware of the vested interests behind such 'reporting', but also to ask themselves what they could do about such distortions, and in this way experiencing that individuals can exercise some control over what is happening in their society.

As to the teaching of *literacy*, the *National Literacy Strategy – A Framework for Teaching* (DfEE 1998a) has been the subject of much debate. Fears that have been aired about its perceived straitjacket include 'endless daily analysis and scrutiny' and 'endurance of the same lesson pattern day after day' which will lead to unimaginative teaching and 'crush the will to read'. The letters published in the *Times Educational Supplement* (April to July 1998) from which these extracts are taken, continue to criticise the NLS: 'learning about words and sentences and isolating literacy as a separate subject via one imposed methodology is unsuitable for children at the extremes of ability', 'compelling teachers to ignore the varying developmental needs that exist in any class', 'a recipe for further disaffection for those already disadvantaged' and 'prohibiting spending time on exploring ideas'. Others, admitting these dangers as real, suggest, however, that it does not condemn teachers to teaching words in arid isolation but, 'done well, could represent high quality interaction between teacher and child and concentrate access to skills' (Griffiths 1998), letting children explore meanings in context and transfer their knowledge to other situations. A Cambridgeshire project described by Wrenn (1998) uses stories and historical texts about the everyday lives of children in Victorian Britain and letters written in Tudor times that involve pupils in questions about changes in language and vocabulary over the centuries. It explores the creative process of writing, noting words with which to express thoughts, feelings, sensations, which all lead to forms of knowledge. Palmer's literacy hour project 'Rainy Days' (1998) contains texts for sharing 'rainy day words' with younger pupils and 'rainy day wisdom' for older ones. The National Literacy Association (1998) offers material for 'unmasking the Literacy Hour'. Thus Nunes (1998) sees the drive for literacy and numeracy as 'the source of new possibilities, (tools) that can enhance pupils' thinking and develop their minds'.

The 'Framework for Teaching' can then be made to chime in with issues discussed in this chapter. It contains sections which emphasise that 'pupils need to understand that their writing will be read by other people', indicating the importance of relating to others; learning to 'compose a letter' can be linked to a range of study units elsewhere, as to questions in history about how and what people wrote about in past centuries. Allowance is made for a wide range of text materials in fiction, poetry, non-fiction, awareness-raising through 'persuasive writing' for composing adverts and circulars which can be related to good or questionable causes. At Key Stages 1 and 2 this could suggest a foundation for later media studies to increase the ability of using information discriminately.

Similar cross-curricular relevance is suggested by the School Curriculum and Assessment Authority's (1998) investigation into literacy and communication key skills that matter in the workplace, such as skills of self-representation (already developed through schools' Records of Achievement), ability to explain and speak up for oneself non-confrontationally, sharing each other's work experiences, checking information and asking questions about it. Apprentices have to write reports similar to the writing needed for recording science or design and technology work at school.

Early Years teachers, in line with Nunes' (1998) analysis of numbers as objects of thought, report using the post office elements of the Ahlbergs' *Jolly Postman* stories by doubling *mathematics* with work on social skills. Others develop children's insights into numeracy by relating number work to the work of nurses and thus to the extent to which our health depends on their number skills (Hoyles and Neumark 1998). Numeracy skills for the workplace have also been surveyed by the School Curriculum and Assessment Authority (1998). Gorman (1998) looks beyond the prescribed Numeracy Hour to working with the whole class, groups and individuals for sharing strategies in ways that maximise the virtues of teacher–pupil and pupil–pupil interaction, assessing progress and level of understanding as a responsive pedagogue who knows how to encourage rather than just praise or admonish.

Others argue that *mathematics* can be taught creatively through references to *sport*, such as calculating a player's understanding of *geometry* when he scored a goal by kicking the ball so accurately that it found its way into the small gap which separated the defender and a post(!), or just adding up the costs of supporting a particular team; and that there are possibilities even in teaching *statistics* to raise awareness of people's feelings and awaken empathy ('what might it be like to be one of those statistics?', 'can one do something about these?'). Teachers listing the cross-curricular opportunities of mathematics include *art* (study of decorative motifs across the centuries and different cultural traditions, expressing their ethical philosophies and life stances), modern day travel (exchange rates, flight times, weather conditions, logos, designs of travel brochures) and the mathematics of daily life's probabilities (from winning the lottery to 'Murphy's Law').

As the 1998 World Cup fever demonstrated, *Sport* itself, can become a similarly all-embracing subject when teachers address their pupils' emotional and social realities. They could discuss reactions to World Cup events, coping with winning and losing in sport and in life, how people expressed their feelings, the words they used when 'England didn't make it' (gutted, choked, distraught, heartbroken); their reactions to individuals' misfortune (Beckham, Ronaldo) with questions about empathy: what is meant by 'being a good sport'? 'What about the problems of celebrities (Gazza, Collymore) when their egos feel threatened, language fails them and they hit out at those closest to them? What will players feel during penalty shoot-outs? Did you hear about the boy who at the 1996 Eurocup so identified with Southgate when his penalty miss lost England the match that he wrote him a comforting letter? What did *you* feel? Could you write such a letter? Can you imagine writing a report about such a match, either as winner or loser? Did you notice differences in the participating countries' reactions to events of the World Cup?'

Similarly, *foreign language* teachers, like their *English* colleagues, found World Cup events conducive to thinking of simple phrases for making friends with people from other countries and to stimulate wider interests. They were able to include discussion of issues like patriotism versus nationalism ('How true is it that 'a patriot loves his own country, a nationalist hates others?'); the effect of a victorious multi-ethnic team who gave their best in spite of the racism they had hitherto experienced in France; awareness about what makes people move to another country and what they are hoping for, what they find, what their new country may gain. There is then an obvious potential for language work as well as social awareness in tasks like writing a story starting 'When I stepped off the boat...'.

Teachers found that pupils became thoughtful when asked what it means to them to be 'English', to list their own country's characteristics to be proud of, and that they may need some coaching to include 19th century engineering skills for shipbuilding and railways, progress in medicine, education, the arts, as they may when asked about sport as capable of displaying *moral values* (sportsmanship, teamwork, being good losers, competition only within value boundaries) – and to think of the opposites of these as perhaps damaging them personally. Youth workers (see also Chapter 7 on interagency cooperation) now warn about this dark side of disaffected youths' identification with those qualities reflected in sport which excluded them from the classroom, where their problems could have been 'heard' when still manageable, where these could have been taken seriously. Experiencing school as irrelevant to their concerns, however, they were not learning how to control aspects of their life and 'became uncontrollable, [with] contemporary sport a refuge and magnet for dysfunctional men who opted for a programme of perpetual puerility' (Dakers 1998). According to Phillips (1998) many teenage boys are 'just not daring to work harder for fear of being laughed at but at heart want success', and then perceive the teachers as 'favouring the more hard-working girls'.

There are growing concerns about 'writing boys off' in their first term because of their apparently poorer performance compared to that of girls, with baseline-assessing Local Councils relegating twice as many boys as girls to the bottom attainment category (Thornton 1998). Dixon (1998) warns that their eventually turning their backs on learning for good may well begin here, when exuberant five- and six-year-olds, facing a decreasing range of physical activities, physical frustration and subsequent restlessness and lack of attention, may be seen as 'a tiresome liability [and] start to be called "inattentive", "uncooperative", "lazy", and react by conforming to such descriptions', instead of schools turning their exuberance to educational advantage, allowing them to express what they see as relevant to their lives, as a gradual introduction to academic learning.

In the consultative groups, teachers agreed that, like all subjects, the *sciences*, too, need to be taught in personally significant ways, in relation to human attitudes and values about people and things around them (see Black *et al.* (1996) about safety and ethical practices in the workplace). For an impressive example of teachers at a children's hospital school taking hospital science into the classrooms of local primary schools and then bringing their children back into the hospital, see Aggarval and McGonagle (1996). Together, the children here learn what happens inside a hospital, are able to use 'let's pretend' plastic toy models of medical instruments for blood pressure and pulse metering, are allowed to wear bandages and learn about what happens inside their bodies. The teachers can link this with National Curriculum themes like 'processes of life'. On the personal and social side, the children on the wards have a chance to mix with others from outside the hospital, while those from the local schools, seeing the inside of a hospital and meeting medical staff, can be helped to develop confidence, which 'ought to help allay their fears' (Aggarval and McGonagle 1996).

Being taught in personally significant ways, pupils can begin to realise the human drama behind scientific discovery and knowledge gained through endeavour by people who needed to solve and communicate problems with which they were faced, just as the pupils are. Finding out about ourselves, the limitations and potential with which we come into the world (we cannot spin webs but we can learn to use language and our minds!) can heighten children's curiosity, interest and respect for themselves as learners and can develop their potential for self-understanding, social involvement (the means by which our capacities are developed or denied) and responsibility (powerfully expressed in Michael Frayn's recent play *Copenhagen*.

Teachers of *geography*, *history* and *social studies* similarly considered how best to relate their subjects to the pupils' concerns, rather than just covering a syllabus 'out there'. Like their science colleagues, they felt that an awareness of the impact of geographical, historical and social factors on human activities, and the skills, attitudes and language of enquiry and interpretation of evidence which they tried to teach within their disciplines, were equally appropriate to their pupils' daily lives and relationships.

Relating subject language to basic themes in life and learning

Opportunities to relate subject language to the 'basic themes which give form to life and learning' (Bruner 1968) exist throughout school life, helping children to deal with problems they may be facing when leaving school, and to face the threatening as well as the hopeful aspects of the adult world of relationships, work and non-work, leisure and parenthood.

Through collaborative consultancy, however, teachers experience themselves both as *learners* and as *teachers*, capable of contributing to their colleagues' and their own effectiveness. Being assisted in using enabling consultancy skills with each other, they become more aware of how language processes can optimise learning. In sharing their complementary experience in non-judgemental supportive language, they maximise their expertise and discover strengths on which to build. They also offer each other – through being listened to and feeling cared about – creative professional support and an emotional refuge when things seem to be going wrong.

Language processes, however, can also disturb communication and limit understanding, the effects of which teachers became aware of in their explorations. They noticed occasions when their own use of language seemed judgemental (through the 'Have you thought of...?' kind of closed question) and that they were, at such moments, not *learning from each other*. Articulating these language experiences when they occur makes it easier to understand what is meant by *learning from one's pupils*, in the way that a mother can learn from her infant 'how to speak to him so that he can learn' (Lewis 1963). It is widely accepted that the effectiveness of workers in the caring professions depends on their responsiveness to the client's communication and their ability to adapt to the needs that he expresses. Teachers agreed that it is equally profitable for them to consider their ways of speaking to children in this context of susceptibility and accessibility (see Hart 1996), to recognise which language and negotiating patterns are enabling and which are liable, unintentionally, to close learning situations or to damage learning relationships, but they also found that they themselves needed the support which they were receiving, to reactivate their abilities to apply this understanding in their day-to-day teaching.

There is then a considerable potential in gearing the ordinary curriculum to those 'basic themes' which Bruner (1968) explored as 'giving form to life and learning', attending to its inherent emotional and social factors, not for offering children a substitute for missing experience but for providing those 'educational opportunities of quality' (Rutter 1991; see also Warnock 1996) which help to pave their pathways into adulthood. As teachers agree, offering these opportunities at every level of attainment and age through subjects and learning activities across even a formal curriculum enriches that curriculum.

This requires teachers who can appreciate these themes and the part that they have played in their own development, and who understand the framework of relationships which enable children to learn. Thus integrated, these themes become a potent help in the search for excellence. In collaborative consultancy exploration we need only draw attention to the existence and importance of these themes in the general educational programme. As we have seen, the consultant's task is not to offer an alternative curriculum but an approach in which these themes – suggested by teacher educators in this and other countries for a good part of this century – are activated in the teachers' minds. The approach gives depth to learning experiences, whether they are designed for the whole class or considered essential in the specific case, in the pursuit of excellence for all.

Chapter 6

The Home and the School: Collaboration with Parents

The White Paper on excellence in schools strongly emphasises that 'Parents play a crucial role in helping their children learn' (DfEE 1997a) and promotes close collaboration between teachers and parents. Baseline assessments, home–school agreements on fostering reading and numeracy, supporting homework, ensuring regular school attendance: all are – in the words of the Under Secretary of State for School Standards – geared to 'encouraging parents to get involved with their children's school career at the earliest possible opportunity...[and to] encouraging the all important dialogue between home and school' (Clarke, C., MP 1998).

However, there are fears, that
- the new baseline assessment procedures could play a part in determining ability bands and therefore encourage parents to coach their children in order to avoid their being branded as failures at the age of school entry;
- some parents may perceive home–school agreements as compulsory contracts (both terms are used synonymously in the White Paper), which, for many parents, may mean 'having to sign something you can't deliver, [which] will increase the isolation of parents who know that they are failing and may be powerless to prevent it' (Sallis 1996);
- while 'compulsory parental involvement in reading could stifle a child's enjoyment' (Williams 1998); and
- 'mothers (from poorer families) are too intimidated by schools and teachers to ask for help with their children's learning' (Ghouri 1998).

In contrast, a discussion in the *Times Educational Supplement* centred on a parent who didn't want to be seen as 'pushy' and decided not to tell the reception class teacher about her daughter's 'giftedness'. What were this parent's fears if the 'secret' were discovered? And might the child sense her mother's worry and keep the secret and 'conform to the class norm by pretending that she can't read, pretend not to know the answers to questions, hold back from classroom discussion' (Freeman 1996)?

How confident are parents to meet teachers in what one mother referred to as that 'no-man's-land between home and school, a minefield strewn with explosive emotions and prejudice'? How good are schools at sharing their knowledge with parents? For decades, at least, close cooperation between home and school has been stressed as important. The White Paper now reminds schools that parents need accurate information and regular feedback about what is happening in schools, and that parents should be given an effective voice for underpinning the partnerships which all schools are now required to build.

True partnership implies mutual respect. It implies a recognition of a joint endeavour to which both parties have something to contribute. However, both teachers and parents can still experience meetings as a source of stress if they do not have the necessary skills to approach each other with confidence. In the consultancy sessions, teachers became aware of how their relationships with parents are affected by how both sides view each other and the child's progress.

Teachers may underestimate parents' ability to appreciate the teacher's efforts to help their child, or may see a seemingly poor parent–child relationship, parental problems, lack of understanding, hostility to teachers or apparent apathy as causing the child's difficulties (in Ivan's case (pp. 15–17) parents' worries about their handicapped child seemed to have made them unaware of their healthy child's problems at school) and as impeding cooperation. *Parents* may fear that they are being judged when they meet teachers, and that the impression they make could influence their child's treatment at school, and so may be reluctant to disagree with the teacher, especially if, at parents' evenings, long queues and minimal privacy lead to reluctance to make further individual appointments to discuss an issue. Their reluctance can then be mistaken for lack of interest. Parents may accuse the school of being at the root of the child's lack of progress, and may complain that the teachers give their child too little, too much, or the wrong kind of attention. However, they may themselves be anxious and seek an interview with the school but fail to get the advice that they hoped for, or to act on that given. They may be at a loss for words with teachers who are unaware of how communication between them has broken down or could be improved. Teachers will then fail to obtain the kind of information which might enable them to understand the child's and parents' situation better and may be unable to explain even to those willing to cooperate how to motivate reluctant children to become constructively involved.

On the other hand, teachers have been known, indirectly, to help parents improve their relationships with each other and between them and their children at home and so benefit progress at school (see the conversations described on p. 93). Teachers could raise parents' awareness about children's need for special attention during crucial transition periods like the first year of secondary school, to notice when things may be going wrong (in line with Lanyado (1989), comparing it to the attention one gives to a toddler who is just learning to walk).

Sociologists and psychologists examining the socio-psychodynamic aspect of professional relationships have directed attention to the frequent breakdown of parent–teacher relationships, especially when meetings take place over a child's difficulty. There are hazards in communication and cooperation created by suggestions of power and influence, omniscience or partiality, whether assumed by one side or attributed to it by the other. If there are problems to be discussed, parents feel a particular need for support but may also be specially vulnerable in the face of professionals who may appear to define their child exclusively in terms of the difficulty or may seem to attribute blame to the parents. Parents may feel intimidated or threatened by well-meaning, but perhaps ambivalent, professionals who may not be aware of these feelings, and instead perceive parents as being inarticulate or inadequate, who feel anxious or guilty for their suspected part in the child's difficulty. As Dowling and Osborne (1994) show from the perspective of a 'joint systems approach', the influence of the two systems upon each other in relation to a child's problem affects the problem itself. Thus Mittler and Mittler (1982) point out that teachers, like social workers, need to be aware of the child in the context of his family as a whole (the DfEE White Paper (1997a) emphasises the role of the wider family in children's learning), and to take into consideration these influences which affect a child's progress (notice how Len's teachers (pp. 48–51) were helped in their group to understand the inter generational pressures at work in the family). Teachers thus need to possess and *to apply as teachers* some of the knowledge and skills of social workers in working with families.

Research into parent involvement notes how insufficiently developed such skills are in teachers. Teachers frequently appear unaware that they themselves can learn from parents (Tizard and Hughes 1984), that work with parents is likely to be more effective if built on their 'equivalent expertise' and understanding (Pugh *et al.* 1994, Wolfendale 1983) and that with recognition and encouragement of their potential and actual strengths parents are more likely to encourage those of their children. Even at the stage of nursery education, where a large proportion of parents are in daily contact with staff, it has been found that the staff may mistake their cordial relationships with parents for genuine parent involvement. There was in fact little exchange of information, although both sides said that they would like to have more information from each other, and very little real cooperation. Misconceptions on both sides seemed to be preventing better communication: parents felt unable to ask the questions that they would have liked to ask and teachers thought parents uninterested.

A picture, then, emerges of well-intentioned efforts and of obstacles to be overcome if a home–school partnership is to achieve the conjoint support which the government's drive towards excellence for all now suggests.

When teachers in their groups examined their contacts with parents, they agreed that, on the one hand, they may well underrate them, disapprove, talk at them, fear to get too involved and then give too ready reassurance, which may in fact close the communication rather than reassure and that, on the other hand, parents may feel overtaxed by demands they cannot meet. (Mittler warns teachers against suggesting to parents a parenting style too alien for them to follow.) They also found that worries and uncertainties, due to socio-economic circumstances or to the parents' own childhood scars, may make a school's request to meet them feel like another threat. The teachers agreed that in all such cases there was something they could do to ease the situation, at least about the style of meeting and the first small steps towards dialogue. Realising that their own preconceptions, judgements and reactions often proved a hindrance, they found it useful to examine these in relation to the case discussed.

Wherever it was relevant in a specific case discussion, teachers were able to consider what can take place 'between the words' when parents and teachers meet, what facts, feelings and fantasies may ease or disturb a meeting and what fears, anxieties or expectations may disturb and distort the intended communication. They could then explore what professional skills were needed to achieve the common objective of the meeting, which was that it should be of help to the child concerned. Clearly, such encounters should be reasonably pleasant for the parent. The teachers therefore needed to think about the feelings that parents may have about themselves as parents or about their children when they face a teacher and what feelings they may have about the authority assumed by others. They had to consider that parents may or may not wish to express the anxieties and resentments which can be aroused if they feel that their child is not liked, or unfairly treated, or if the teachers seem to assume that they know what is good for him. If parents doubt the teacher's quality or interest in the child, they may be worried about his future; unacknowledged doubts about their own adequacy as parents may be intensified by envy of a competent teacher or by fear of his or her rivalry.

Teachers confirmed that they have, as we have seen, various reactions to parental behaviour. They may be in considerable turmoil when they meet parents who appear to them to be failing their children and to find no joy in them and who reiterate hostile feelings about the child; this can make teachers fear further contacts, lest anything they say may be used against the child at home, as we saw in Teresa's case (pp. 24–7). They meet parents in conflict with each other in which the children get involved, others united against a child and yet others who 'want the best' for him but seem to set about it in ways which undermine his progress. They may hear parents praise one child to the skies and have no good word for his brother or sister. Teachers will naturally not know what deep-seated causes may have led to this rejection. Moreover, they may also not sufficiently understand the processes through which children contribute to the interaction between parents and children in such a way that some children come to be perceived as 'good', treated lovingly and behave affectionately in return and others elicit constant irritability and hostility from parents who cannot tolerate or adjust to their needs in a vicious spiral of bad feelings, where the parents need as much support as the children. Teachers will also know nothing of the damaged childhood which causes some parents to induce their children to re-enact their own early battles with teachers and the unjust world that they seem to represent; they cannot make allowances for what they do not know, but they can learn to suspect some such reason for parental hostility. Parents may even blame the child's bad behaviour for their own marital difficulties or seem to hold the teachers responsible. In Vic's case (pp. 32–5) the teachers could see this as an indication of the mother's need for support rather than for the blame or rejection she seemed to expect. Len's grandmother (pp. 48–51) directed great anger at his teachers who at first saw no chance of mollifying her, but her feelings towards them changed when they themselves ceased to reject her and saw her as a worried and suffering woman who herself needed acceptance and support. In another case it was possible to overcome a grandmother's hostile feelings to her ten-year-old granddaughter (whom she singled out as being like the hated daughter-in-law who had abandoned the family, leaving the grandmother to look after the children) when the teacher mentioned how much the girl needed a caring grandmother's help and how good it was for her to have this granny, thereby implying confidence in the grandmother in spite of her hostile feelings – an approach to the partnership relationship analysed by Irvine (1979) as both insight-promoting and strengthening caring capacity.

If teachers want to meet parents as partners, they need to be aware of such pressures, but also to be careful not to interfere with a complex system of relationships outside their scope or mandate, as Rutter (1975) warns. They also need to avoid a defeatist view of their own and the parents' capabilities. As research suggests (Quinton and Rutter 1983, 1988; Quinton 1987) adverse conditions may or may not seriously affect parenting abilities, and the childhood deprivations of parents may be perpetuated or attenuated by later experiences of criticism or support, including that received from teachers. Whether teachers manage to initiate a supportive relationship or unwittingly collude with the parents' negative expectations, will at least in part depend on their own understanding of such issues and their reactions to parents' behaviour.

Teachers in the groups found it helpful to examine in general terms (i.e. without individual exposure) how easy it is to judge parents without full understanding, to see teacher–parent relationships in one-way terms of experts giving advice to laymen and to fear that lay people will find them wanting and reject or attack their authority.

Teachers could see how this defeated their aims by reinforcing or creating the gulf that they were trying to bridge. We considered the ambivalence which any one of us may feel about getting involved beyond our traditional professional boundaries and how we may take defensive stances against defensive parents, so failing to note their anxiety and to take account of their experience. Teachers could accept that, if we feel defensive about our own human insufficiencies, these feelings can make us a convenient target for a parent's anger or anxiety.

However, if we accept such insufficiencies, we are more likely to be able to deal with them and to understand and accept those of the parents, no matter how repugnant they may sometimes seem at first. Instead of seeing a parent as totally uncaring, ungrateful or unreasonably demanding, teachers found that it helped to consider that the feelings aroused in them might be a reflection of the parents' own feelings and that the parents might themselves experience others as uncaring, ungrateful and over-demanding. This made it easier for the teachers to accept the parents, and to get in touch with their caring abilities, by manifesting a caring professional attitude towards them.

It seemed to be generally more helpful to work on some assumptions rather than on others; that parents have and can develop skills and that they care (this should be assumed even about blatantly rejecting parents, as Kahn and Wright (1980) stress in their discussion of the universality of rejection and the hidden acceptance in rejecting families); that parents want their children to get on and would like to get on with them; that, where they seem to hinder or not to understand, parents may respond to the teachers' awareness of their children's needs and their emphasis on the parents' importance to their children (a crucial point to make explicit as we saw in Michael's and Len's cases (pp. 30–32 and 48–51); that parents are better involved by hearing good news about their children than by the complaints which they may expect; that this is more likely to convince parents that the teacher is on their child's side and on theirs.

It was possible to help teachers to accept the parents' feelings – even, or especially, where these seemed to be directed against the child. Teachers found that, if parents with such negative feelings hear a head teacher or any teacher who has first accepted the parents, speak well of the child whom they had so far singled out for the difficulties that he or she was 'causing' them, this sometimes helped them to take a better view of themselves and of the child (as had happened in the case of Dave (pp. 35–8) and of the grandmother just described).

Teachers thus appreciated that parents need opportunities to express their feelings and to find them understood and accepted by somebody who is helpful, non-judgemental, on their side and confident about their importance to their child. This helped the teachers to lower tensions, to reduce a parent's sense of injustice and to discuss with them how parents and children influence each other and how the pressures faced by parents – their lack of time, fears about employment or loss of job, and other family anxieties – can perhaps be coped with in such a way that their children are freer to concentrate on school work and not fall behind because of what worries the parents. Talk about their children's needs at school and how playing with them at home and talking and listening to them can help, enabled the teachers to invite the parents' help as being important also to the teacher. Teachers were surprised to find how thrilled parents often were when their help was invited and at times sensed that, while they were discussing with a parent how they might together help a child (for instance in relating better to other children), they were also helping the parent with a similar difficulty (learning to relate better to other adults with whom contact had been a nightmare). (As we saw (p.71), similar developments occurred between consultant and teachers and were recognised as a particular feature of the Caplan model of consultation.) They found that such support often gave new confidence, especially to single custodial mothers or fathers, who feared that they might not be able to cope on their own. There was no need to probe into privacy or underlying causes, or to exhort parents, and thereby to undermine their sense of authority. Information-seeking questions could at the same time contain oblique dashes of advice ('what are the things that you can be nice about with him at home?' or 'how does she react if you say something good about her while you are busy with baby?') and sometimes elicited further light on what was wrong as well as pointing the way to its amelioration, without becoming didactic about the need to show love more openly or how to deal with discipline problems by setting limits as well as giving encouragement.

It was important, however, for teachers always to understand partnership as a reciprocal process and not to misunderstand it as a one-way process of offering parents information and requesting their help. Such information about the teacher's objectives regarding the child, how particular difficulties are being handled, how the child responds to this at school and how the parent might support the teacher's efforts at home (such as commenting encouragingly and trying to refrain from disparaging remarks) is clearly an important part of parent–teacher cooperation and can have impressive effects on children's self-concept and school achievement. Partnership, however, also requires understanding of what teachers can learn from parents about children at home (Tizard and Hughes, 1984); respect for the parents' experience; and readiness to learn from the parents' knowledge of their children, how they see their child's needs and strengths, how they feel that these needs might best be met and what they feel they can contribute to this joint endeavour – especially so when parents feel overwhelmed by their difficulties.

Most of the family problems which the teachers mentioned had to do with the parents' own most deeply felt human experiences. Birth, illness and death in the family, upheavals in relationships through family break-up, unemployment or imprisonment of a parent, or a sibling sent away to residential school because of severe emotional/behavioural difficulties or physical handicap are stressful events for child and parents and always entail a change in parental response to the child. In any of these, the teacher's unobtrusive informed support of parent and child can make the difference between coping and greater disturbance.

As we saw with Tony (pp. 19–24), children frequently 'know what they are not supposed to know and feel what they are not supposed to feel' (Bowlby 1979) concerning a lost parent, whose loss they may not be allowed to mention to the parent who remains. This parent may disown the secret, prevaricate about the absence, 'forbid' the child to grieve, try to discredit the absent parent or prevent all talk about him or her. Such a loss, worsened by the parent's feelings, has been shown to be potentially harmful, as the child tries to shut away what is thus forbidden, which persists, however, and may impair his relationships and progress and lead to a sense of unreality, inhibition of curiosity and distrust of others. Evidence shows (Bowlby 1979, Black 1983, Goldacre 1980, 1985) that support for child and parent can prevent some of these consequences if both are helped to share their distress and not distort communication between them.

Increasingly, teachers found that they could give at least some such support without crossing their professional boundaries or getting closer to the parents than either could bear without discomfort. In the case of two children in one teacher's class of eight-year-olds, the opportunity came when the mother of one of them told the teacher of her attempts to refuse access to the father – whose 'bad blood' she blamed for her daughter's unmanageable behaviour – and when the girl had started to taunt and deride a boy in her class for not having a father. This boy was denied all knowledge of his father, in spite of actual contact with the paternal family, whom he was not supposed to know. Both these attempts to obliterate the 'bad' parent were discussed in the group. The teacher and head teacher were able to help the mothers to accept that children want to know about their parents, want to be able to feel good about both of them and that this can improve their self-esteem and self-confidence and lessen the danger that a child will begin later to identify with the image of a 'bad' parent. In other cases, mothers agreed that they might need to reassure their child that the father had not left because of the child's naughtiness. Parent and teacher could then share incidents of difficult behaviour and how they might both treat it with patience instead of adding to it by fighting the child. Teachers were heartened to see how the school's support and a show of trust in the parent's ability to help the child to pull through often kindled in the parents a new enjoyment of their children.

Much of the research on the impact of divorce on children and families and the work of the conciliation agencies are concerned with the question of how to help both the custodial and the non-custodial parent to assist the children 'survive' the break-up. While teachers have no mandate as conciliators, the support which they can give is clearly more than minimal. When new relationships had to be formed with formal or informal step-parents, teachers were able to help both parents and step-parents to become more constructively involved in a child's education. This Ferri (1984) suggests as being within a teacher's remit. They could assist distraught adults to accept that children may have conflicting feelings of jealousy or anger against the newcomer for having 'stolen' or usurped their parent's love and to think of ways of helping them to cope with this. As we saw with Vic (pp. 32–5), a step-parent may be unable to tolerate the child's difficult behaviour, especially if it becomes the cause of discord, and the child may test the ever-diminishing tolerance in his world, at home and at school, in search of some acceptance of his 'badness'. In Vic's case, the school was enabled to break the vicious circle and could give support to both Vic and his despondent mother.

In Jeanie's case (pp. 38–41) we saw how a teacher helped a foster-mother who feared that she was failing the child, by sharing their experience of her. In another family the absence of a disabled child at residential school so dominated every aspect of life that only a talk with their other child's teacher helped them to realise the support he also needed. In a number of cases such as Dave's (pp. 35–8) the family differentiated between the favourite child and another, who was made to carry the family's frustrations. The selection of children for particular family roles is clearly, as Rutter (1975) has stressed, not something which teachers can discuss with parents. Awareness of such possibilities, however, has guided teachers' discussions with parents and helped them to make some parents more accepting. Studies suggest (Madge 1983, Breakwell *et al.* 1984), that even the effects of paternal unemployment – with the increased risks of material hardship, illness, depression and tensions in the family, fears of being despised and depreciated by the outside world – might be mitigated through an 'intellectual ambulance service provided by teachers, family doctors and psychologists' (Brock 1984). For instance, fathers can be alerted to the good effects which the opportunity of better interaction with their children can have on their learning.

Joint exploration in the back-up groups thus confronts teachers with a wide range of home situations affecting a child's progress at school, and with as wide a range of obstacles in the path of parent–teacher partnership. They saw that many of these, often seen as beyond a teacher's scope, can still be influenced in support of the child if teachers know how to share their concern without intrusion, recognise parents as people with anxieties of their own but also with actual and potential strengths which need to be encouraged, and do not appear to define the child exclusively in terms of his or her difficulties. As we have seen, teachers were often surprised by the relative ease with which some parents, whom they had thought to be entrenched and immovable, responded to their suggestion of an exchange of information and the teachers' belief in them and their children.

To achieve this quality in the partnership, teachers needed to become more aware of the obstacles which might interfere from either side and to apply their insights to overcoming them through quite specific skills, as it was possible to consider them in the support groups. Caspari (1974) summarised the skills required as:

- showing parents that teachers need their knowledge and help, to enable the teachers to be of maximum help to their child;
- sharing with the family that information which the parents seem able to accept, and encouraging them to comment from their own experience of the child;
- conveying that their concerns are recognised and shared.

If this is sensitively done, parents may see:

- how another adult relates to their child, which suggests how they could themselves relate to him, yet is sufficiently different, because of its professional context, not to be felt as a criticism of their own parental behaviour;
- that the teacher accepts their child as growing up and as capable of acquiring skills;
- that the teacher's care includes them, with their own needs and difficulties, as well as the child;
- that their active participation is enlisted in such a way that they experience some success and a new sense of effectiveness with their children.

It may seem as if teachers were expected to spend an excessive amount of time with parents, time which they cannot normally spare. However, the teachers in the groups did not necessarily spend more time than usual with parents but used their encounters more purposefully to establish an effective partnership. Such meetings were no longer left to chance, as had sometimes been the case, or to the initiative of anxious or irate parents, and the parents were approached with special care, so that they were less likely to feel summoned. Systematic exploration in the groups of what this implied led, as we saw, to better consultation with parents about their children's needs. Instead of ignoring the parents' experience, the teachers began to suggest how both sides might work together, each within their own possibilities, to help the child to progress. In the process, the parent, too, could receive unobtrusive support and could reciprocate the goodwill that was being demonstrated.

All schools will now be aware that special skills are required to build the strong partnerships with parents which are called for in the White Paper on excellence in schools. To be effective, teachers need to understand the partnership agreement as part of a reciprocal process and not misunderstand it as a one-way process of demanding help from parents. Home–school agreements will work best where both parties are involved in the process of composing them. Parents may indeed need 'tips' on how to engage in enjoyable numeracy games with their children or how to read with them (such as talking about the text rather than merely decoding words) or that fathers reading to their sons may thereby forestall boys' literacy problems. Such suggestions will not harm a reciprocal relationship if teachers are able to show respect for the parents' experience (and understand where parents may lack confidence in their ability to help) and readiness to learn from the parents' knowledge of their child, asking information-seeking questions such as what they feel they can contribute to their joint endeavour, rather than merely telling them what they should do. Commenting encouragingly and trying to refrain from dismissive remarks are clearly an important part of parent–teacher cooperation and can have impressive effects on children's self-concept and school achievement.

The teachers also found that joint explorations such as these seemed to enhance their negotiation and partnership skills in general, both with colleagues and with professionals external to the school. Jeanie's (pp. 38–41) and Len's (pp. 48–51) case discussions had confronted them with the hazards of disharmony and conflict that may arise between the guidance and welfare services. It was in the nature of our discussions that the initiative to address and overcome these hazards came from the education side since that was where the staff development programme had been initiated. However, we must also examine the obstacles to effective collaboration across the boundaries of the education, social and health services, at a time when such collaboration has become a matter of urgency. This is the theme of the next chapter.

Chapter 7

Cooperation Between Institutions and Services: Crossing Professional Boundaries

Most professionals will be aware that many children and young people experience a complex range of educational and social problems, that these problems tend to be treated in isolation, and that answers to them lie in breaking down boundaries between the services (Roaf and Lloyd 1995) and between school, work and the community (Hillman 1998).

New government proposals for interagency cooperation are geared to creating a system of integrated working relationships through 'joint training, involving staff from all relevant agencies, as an effective way of promoting shared understanding' (*Working Together*, Department of Health 1998). One of the chief targets stated is 'the promotion of healthy schools as the area of greatest potential to tackle the inequalities set in childhood'. However, the Joseph Rowntree Foundation reminds us, on the one hand, how new such a jointly facilitating approach is to teachers and school management, and that this 'requires additional elements in teacher training', and on the other hand, that 'agencies may not welcome collaboration, especially where they have lost territory to education' (Ball 1998). Lacey and Lomas (1993) refer to the need of developing, for teachers, 'a whole set of new skills, knowledge and understanding', including an understanding of reasons for wanting to resist proposed changes.

Aware of the difficulties, the White Paper on excellence for all children states its plans to overcome 'the barriers to improved collaboration between LEAs, social services and health authorities' and announces its intention also to 'explore ways of changing the balance of work for EPs, so that they can use their expertise as productively as possible' (DfEE 1997b).

Earlier research into multi-agency work by the Joseph Rowntree Foundation (Roaf and Lloyd 1995) shows the extent to which the lack of structured coordination between the services still limits their effectiveness. 'Do Child Care Specialists Understand?' was the question in a mother's account (Roberts 1995) of the distressingly unhelpful attitudes her initially only slightly handicapped son and his parents encountered in their contact with the range of professionals – teaching, medical, psychological, psychiatric – enlisted to help when, after having done well at school until the age of nine, his difficulties became more pronounced. In her foreword to this harrowing book, Mary Warnock finds cause to deplore the 'crass failure of imagination' which some professionals (including teachers) can sometimes display.

In Chapter 3 we saw how a collaborative training structure can help to prevent such failure within the school. We shall now examine the extent to which it can help to enable individual teachers, trained in the collaborative communication skills we have been discussing, to promote effective cooperation across the services.

For decades, successive governments have criticised professional isolation while educational associations published guidelines and ran conferences on how professionals should play a fuller role within multidisciplinary teams. As more cases of tragic neglect of children came to light, books by practitioners (Fitzherbert 1977) urged teachers and social workers to include each other in their recognition of problems which need to be solved jointly. Researchers in training departments (Kolvin *et al.* 1982, Evans 1990) reported on their projects and courses for developing multiprofessional and interagency cooperation and highlighted the importance of sharing ideas and information about each other's roles and responsibilities to encourage cooperation. Mere encouragement to do so, however, had left local authorities to the mercy of their level of awareness. As Evans warns, even where the structures for cooperation exist, lack of understanding and of a real appreciation of its importance may impede its implementation, as different departments fail to inform each other of their procedures, fail to address their disparate expectations and fail to address the fragmentation even within their own professions.

As has been detailed elsewhere (Hanko 1989b, 1991), the fragmentation within the education profession has its own dysfunctional barriers, believing them to make for easier management. A process that should be perceived as continuous for each child is thus split into discontinuous stages. To diminish its effects, individual schools have been increasing their efforts to soften the discontinuity through joint projects between primary and secondary schools and between special settings and mainstream schools. An example is the science project already referred to (see Chapter 5 and Aggarval and McGonagle 1996) developed by teachers of the Chelsea Children's Hospital School, well versed in making use of a collaborative approach. By involving the multidisciplinary team, parents and local schools in joint science workshops, they are 'making education an integral part of the overall treatment and the school an essential component of the hospital's service' (Steel and Ofield 1998).

We saw how in some of our case discussions the junior school managed to bridge the divide between stages of schooling by inviting colleagues from the infant and secondary stages to join their group. At secondary level, our support arrangements ensured interdepartmental participation. The hierarchical and managerial fragmentation into different departments could thus be minimised, and any stereotyping distinctions between 'normal' and 'problem children', or the splitting of needs into either educational or behavioural (often omitting attention to emotional factors altogether), could be addressed as they occurred. Staff with their specific responsibilities in subdivisions for separate subjects, pastoral care and special needs' issues learnt no longer to ignore what many had seen exclusively as 'somebody else's business' – a frequent cause of that 'failure of imagination' deplored by Warnock.

With Jeanie's (pp. 38–41) and Len's (pp. 48–51) case discussions, reflective joint exploration helped the staff to recognise not only the nature of the barriers that confronted them but also the ease with which we reinforce them through defensive positions we may take when our efforts at communicating are misunderstood, distorted or snubbed. In Jeanie's case the group discussion structure helped both teacher and social worker not to let the tension between them escalate, and to arrive instead at a solution that was in Jeanie's best interest and reassured her anxious foster mother. Len's school succeeded in furthering his interest by bridging the divide between an anxious parent figure and the Guidance Service she dreaded, while the supportive attitude of her son's school had helped Vic's mother (see pp. 32–5) to find a way to resolve the strife at home that so interfered with his progress at school.

In these cases the teachers had become aware of the barriers that exist against mutual understanding between the professions, and had succeeded in overcoming them within the framework of their own work settings. In Ivan's case (pp. 15–17) the school had, at least belatedly, become aware of the often unacknowledged needs of siblings when the family is preoccupied with the problems of a handicapped child (barely one in ten of an estimated 50,000 children and teenagers who care for sick or disabled family members have had their own needs, and the hazards that these children so often face, assessed (see Barnett and Parker 1998)). Tony's teacher (pp. 19–24) only learned from the child's own outcry of his turmoil and then became the kind of teacher which children of prisoners feel they need, i.e. ready to listen to one such child's silent scream. 'Over 125,000 children have parents in jail but shame often forces them to hide the fact' (Williams 1998). Could Tony's school have been told earlier what this child may be going through?

Dismantling the 'Berlin Wall': But what then?

Official policy now builds on the recognition that the government itself 'needs to break down the barriers between government departments if we are really going to make a difference' and has launched its Sure-Start scheme where centres for the under eights will have 'access to health visitors, childcare and early learning [so that] the most vulnerable children arrive in school ready to learn' (Blair 1998). But what does removing the barriers between professional services entail for the professionals involved? What skills are required to make this 'dismantling of the "Berlin Wall"' (Flood 1998) effective? What are the hazards of it misfiring? What space is there for individual professionals working in a system that has favoured the existence of such barriers? There are hazards in seeing in this historic event an appropriate analogy for a hopefully straightforward removal of traditional barriers to the mental health services, without also paying attention to possible consequences of the removal. As was pointed out to the House of Commons Health Select Committee (1998), 'we need to think about a much wider range of agencies, [with] education playing a fundamental role' (Wilson 1998).

I had occasion to explore the analogy of the 'Berlin Wall' for its relevance to our multiprofessional concerns, in a lecture I gave at the time (Hanko 1991). I used it to show how insufficient mere dismantling of a barrier can be for solving the problems which the segregation had created. Much more had to be removed and to be overcome than the visible impediment. Developing the metaphor, I pointed to all that barbed wire that had to be rolled back, the waste of the no-man's-land that was now to be turned into fertile ground, the health and safety hazards that had to be attended to where the original growth had been poisoned and mines had been laid to prevent people from crossing. Euphoric when the borders were opened, neither side understood that the expertise that had developed from their disparate past experience could not be simply ignored as irrelevant or in other ways interfered with. Attempted interferences led to new tensions, as misunderstandings prevented the joint expertise that needed to be developed from taking root.

Extending the metaphor into interprofessional relationships, we can see the importance of looking more closely at the 'landscape' that surrounds a barrier on both sides, of exploring the extent of its real or perceived barrenness. How much have we ourselves contributed to the divide? Are we in a seemingly suspicious hurry so that our efforts are misjudged as pointing to vested interests? Have both sides been helped to learn each other's language that had developed from our separate experiences? We may misinterpret as deliberate unwillingness what may be due to an inability to 'hear' the other's voice, and remain unaware of our conflicting perceptions. Practitioners in the field (Holditch 1985) have shown the extent to which fraught feelings and entrenched positions as they may arise from such perceptions can lead to poor decisions that appear to the decision-makers as rational and made in the child's best interests.

As we saw in the context of the previous chapters, for collaboration to become effective, team members need to be made aware of such 'aspects of the landscape'. They need to accept that there may be fear or anger on the part of those who may have had a vested interest in the 'Wall', fear of having past insufficiencies brought to the fore, anger at any semblance of missionary zeal for 'wanting to change everything', which would suggest disrespect for their special expertise. The school-based case discussions described showed how a collaborative support structure developed the skills required to convey respect for colleagues' past experience and current perspectives, to be able to note strengths on which to build. Similarly, sharing understanding across the boundaries, while conveying respect for them, is more likely to highlight the mutually enriching complementarity of each profession's particular skills, expertise and expectations.

As interagency programmes concerning young people in danger of becoming disenfranchised from the mainstream of society have shown, schools, social and probation services and the police play an equally important part in jointly addressing issues like truancy and school exclusion (NACRO 1998). As casualties of an excessively competitive teaching climate, such young people cease to value themselves, perceive themselves as having little control over their offending behaviour, use their 'coping' strategies of 'not caring' to mask their low self-esteem and despair. For them, the most important and effective intervention, together with parental involvement, has been to secure an education capable of helping them overcome these difficulties. Devlin's (1997) research with people in prison points to their regrets of not having had the benefit of such intervention. Similar concerns occupy the government's New Start initiative on Engaging Young People in the Learning Society (DfEE 1998b).

The negative consequences of professionals not sharing their complementary expertise add to many children's misery as well as diminish the professionals' own effectiveness. School nurses, with their growing remit for children's mental health, will be better nurses when teachers know how not to marginalise them, as frequently happens. For 'looked-after children in care' teachers will be better teachers if social workers help them to appreciate what it means to grow up in care. Social workers need to be helped in considering the children's educational needs when placing them in care, to be made aware of the effects of frequent changes of address on their educational performance and behaviour in school and on their educational chances, 'locking the educational escape hatch' (Jackson 1987, 1988, 1994; see also Quinton 1987), and the current explosion in school exclusions of 14- to 16-year-olds in public care.

Consistent communication across the divide between teachers and social workers helps both when taking account of findings that children who had been longest in their foster placements tended to be better readers, and of research on 'new parents for older children' (Quinton *et al.* 1990) about how the children's problems are manifested more frequently at schools staffed by teachers with no help in understanding and responding to the children's messages. This highlights what a stressful area that is for new parents under any circumstances, but made worse when neither they nor the teachers know how best to discuss such things with each other, in contrast to Jeanie's situation (pp. 38–41) whose teacher was helped to address a foster mother's anxieties and to prevent escalation of the interprofessional rivalries apparently geared to undermining another professional's competence, and the strong feelings this was arousing. Here, too, supportive joint exploration had helped to secure the equal availability of educational and care skills across the to-be-respected boundaries, assisting all the adults involved as they need to be, for serving the many children of all abilities whom the separate services have failed to serve.

As has been shown, effective multiprofessional collaboration requires the same interprofessional awareness raising that is needed within a monoprofessional work setting. In the words of the NHS Health Advisory Service (1995) Thematic Review, it requires an understanding of 'consultation and liaison processes, to have ready access to all appropriate skills across the current fragmentation, [to ensure] coordinated and integrated child-centred service provision. *Professionals across the services need to practise communication skills* (italics added)…provision of such training need to be integral to all service provision'. We saw in Chapter 3 how Jeanie's and Len's teachers were able to redeploy at a multiprofessional level the skills they were being trained to use with their own colleagues, to the benefit of all involved. They had been enabled to create a climate of cooperation in which it was possible to pool their professional know-how as equals. Insufficient on its own to solve problems which are themselves interprofessional and which cross demarcation lines, it requires complementary enhancement.

We must now turn to these collaborative staff development skills in detail.

Part III

Collaborative Staff Development: Guidelines and Tasks

Developing Collaborative Problem-Solving: Roles and Tasks of Staff Development Tutors

Viewing the landscape

As we have seen, groups to promote professional development can be initiated in very different settings. At secondary school level, Teresa's teacher was meeting only his own colleagues from within the school, all in middle management positions and thus potentially able to act as consultants to their colleagues, to convey to them in their turn the further expertise needed. In contrast, the secondary group which discussed John and Dipak was representative of the whole school and a range of staff experience from senior pastoral care teacher to latest recruit to the profession. In the primary schools, Ivan's, Tony's, Don's, Michael's, Vic's, Dave's and Jeanie's teachers all belonged to groups representing two or more neighbouring schools, covering the whole age range of their pupils, and teachers of a wide range of experience (including secondary school intake staff, who found the discussions of younger pupils equally applicable to the secondary sector, as did the junior school teachers with regard to the secondary and infants staff's contributions). Attendance could last from five weeks to one year, details being carefully negotiated with each school involved.

Examples from these and later groups given in Chapter 3 have shown how, regardless of the setting, consideration of a specific case enabled the consulting staff development tutor to promote among the staff, across departments and hierarchies, exploration of wider issues arising from it. Emotional and social factors were noted as playing a part in children's learning and failure to learn. The significance of seemingly baffling behaviour, the individual needs that it may indicate, what responses to it might be appropriate and the need to understand one's own reaction to the needs expressed and the behaviour displayed are examples of the kind of issues which arose.

We saw what a considerable capital of latent skills and personal resources such explorations can tap in teachers and make available for use in the classroom. Teachers, who were ambivalent about asking for help while expecting to be given advice, welcomed the chance of discovering and deciding for themselves how they might improve a pupil's situation and learning environment. We saw how these processes developed and how their development in the core attenders (who chose to attend the group from first to last with a view to initiating other development groups) benefited short-term members and newcomers who learned from the questions which were being asked in the group on how to look for workable solutions. By extending their knowledge of the way in which situations and backgrounds can affect learning in a specific case, teachers were enabled to relax their hold on preconceived ideas about the child in question and about their own ineffectiveness with him. The group helped them to look with fresh eyes at the situation, to see it also from the pupil's point of view and to respond more adequately to the needs that his behaviour seemed to indicate. We saw how teachers became more objective, regained lost confidence in approaching pupils and were more able to make demands on them in a way which enabled the pupils to begin to meet them.

Developments such as these offer valuable pointers for the advancement of collaborative models for colleagues to draw on and further enhance each other's complementary skills, and for the training of specially assigned members of staff for such work by other professionals. It would extend to all teachers, as part of the school's development plan, some of the expertise already available both within and across schools and school services. On the school staff, there are colleagues with a remit for working with other staff, such as the school's in-service, special needs, pastoral care or curriculum coordinators, mentors charged with the induction of new teachers, or staff from school-based special settings engaged in outreach work. Members of the psychological and education support services, tutors of professional training courses, or independent providers can be enlisted to make their relevant special expertise collaboratively available in such a way that it is of immediate and long-term use to teachers for application in the classroom.

Such developments highlight not only the potential of a collaborative model but also show how readily schools accept it when its remit has been clarified and use is made of the communication channels open to inform staff about it. While complementary expertise can also be shared during informal contacts with individual colleagues (including walking along the school corridor!) or in centre-based training courses, in a school-based course it can be structured as a normal institutional in-service feature of the school's development programme, without the arbitrariness of only some teachers being able to attend an away-course. Evidence shows that pressure of time need not be an obstacle to wider deployment of staff expertise. Early consultation in a group setting has been shown to decrease the pressures on both specially assigned development staff and classroom teachers, which arise from having to teach children whose needs one does not fully understand. The question is not one of extra time but of skill and flexibility in the use of expertise. Each professional willing to share his understanding with groups of other professionals will have his own way of using it. To do so effectively, however, requires special interprofessional skills, based on an understanding of the work setting in which they are to be exercised. It is to these 'aspects of the landscape' that we now turn.

Knowing the stumbling blocks

The work described in these pages, like the original account of the approach (Hanko 1985), developed as a provider's response to a growing need (teaching 'difficult-to-teach' children) in which the teachers had requested support. They did not specify *how* the support might be provided and it was left to the provider to discuss with them, in the light of past experience and research evidence, what type of support was most likely to meet their own professional needs and those of the children that they were worried about. (The original provision had developed as part of a DES-supported two-year Project. Its evaluators referred to this part of the Project as 'a very successful joint course...considered by teachers involved to have been their most worthwhile activity of the two year period' (Baker and Sikora 1982, Hider 1981). Their conclusions about its success related particularly to the detail in which the consulting provider had prepared the schools for the programme). Clarification at the outset is clearly crucial, of what it would and would not be possible to provide, what the teachers might reasonably expect to achieve and what ground rules would have to be honoured in the process. Agreement needs to be reached as to timing, frequency and minimum number of sessions needed to meet these expectations, and the pros and cons of possible options need to be outlined. Decisions about initial and developing group membership likewise must involve the teachers from the beginning in discussing what structure and procedure might be of maximum benefit to the staff as a whole.

As described in Part I, the expertise of the consulting tutor/facilitator was pooled with that of the teachers. Staff specially experienced in the field of children's emotional and behavioural difficulties exist in a range of services and are now being urged – and in the case of school psychologists are increasingly expected (DfEE 1997b) – to share with their colleagues in mainstream schools their expertise and depth of understanding and to equip themselves with the skills required for taking on what will be for many of them a new role. This also applies to the specially qualified pastoral, counselling and other special needs support teachers (paragraph 2.26 of the Code of Practice, DfE 1994) who are arranging staff seminars in their schools, who may start pilot groups with like-minded colleagues willing to talk about current problems, and who hope later to extend these to the rest of the staff. As we have seen, such teamwork with teachers requires from those in a position to develop it an ability to bridge the gap between classroom teachers and those with additional understanding of the emotional and social factors that affect children's learning and to demonstrate that their skills will in fact be of use in the classroom.

The ground for such support work thus needs to be most carefully prepared. For most schools consultative collaboration is a new experience. A potential consultant or staff workshop initiator – whether internal or external – has to keep this in mind to be able to appreciate what difficulties may impede such a new group's work. The findings of group psychology and sociological analysis are useful to consider in this context of involving staff in their own professional development programme. They help to be aware of how influences supporting the professional task may be strengthened, and those which interfere may be reduced (see for instance Bion 1961, Morris 1965, Rice 1971, Taylor 1994). They help to illuminate the values and assumptions concerning interaction and purpose in education which underline collaborative consultancy work.

Of particular concern here are perceptions of the professional task and of the nature of problems and the question of whether and how these perceptions can or should be altered if found to rest on labels and typifications or ideological evaluations dysfunctional to the task. Much has for instance been written to alert teachers to the obstacles with which their own perceptions of pupil behaviour may confront their pupils with regard to self-concept, pupil career, access and opportunity in education and after school, and how value judgements of society are reinforced in schools, but also how the resulting distortions may be redressed if one draws teachers' attention to them. Of special interest here is the fate of innovations in mainstream schools (Clark *et al.* 1997) and the frequency with which, because of social and institutional processes inimical to the change, innovations fail to achieve their aim. It therefore matters that the 'innovator' understands what the changes involve for all concerned and that he does not neglect to teach the skills and to foster the attitudes required to sustain the changes. A staff development tutor needs to consider such matters from the outset. It is important for him to have an idea of what stumbling blocks, hurdles and snags he may encounter on the way and to be prepared to examine, as Mongon and Hart (1989), Hart (1996) have done so effectively, what went wrong if his efforts do not meet the success hoped for.

Abortive developments in my own experience for instance – such as groups which ceased prematurely or failed to take off at all – have retrospectively highlighted several crucial points: I learned that a selective offer to one school alone may suggest a lack of confidence in the staff, which acceptance – as they may fear – seems to confirm. I also found that, while the support of head teacher and senior staff is obviously essential, they may welcome the arrangement but may not appreciate the continuity of internal support required; they may set up competing events, either because they have forgotten when the group meets or because they think it will not matter if some members have to miss a meeting for some other task.

In contrast, I found that an enthusiastic head teacher may welcome the arrangement too readily, which can become counter-productive. In one case, a head teacher arranged for all the staff to attend, and it later emerged that at least some of them were coming unwillingly to comply with the head teacher's obvious wish, and this brought entrenched staffroom tensions into the group. These and similar experiences elsewhere showed that it was essential for the head teacher to offer the arrangement to the staff rather than to appear to impose it or to welcome it too eagerly without sufficient discussion; that external providers need to offer staff development programmes at least on an area basis; that their representative(s) and initiators from among the school staff need to have established credibility in their support of individual colleagues and that there should be no semblance of an obligation on any particular teacher, to avoid suggestions of his being seen as 'in need of help'. However, such groups have also worked well under 'directed time' conditions which by definition leave individual teachers little choice whether or not to attend. Collaborative consultants may find this a good opportunity to use their interprofessional skills with reluctant, unwilling or initially perhaps even hostile participants, and in this way, of course, experience for themselves what is everyday classroom experience for the teachers with whom they are to work.

Initiating a staff development group

(i) First approaches within or to the institution

It is essential to give careful thought to issues such as these regardless of whether the would-be consultant is a specially qualified member of the school staff or comes from outside the institution. Either needs to be aware that he may for instance be misapprehended by some teachers as critical of their methods; this hazard must be tackled when the idea of staff development is first raised. This may come in the form of a question or request from some section or individual in the school. Alternatively, potential consultants may themselves be able to take the initiative by turning their routine contacts with teachers about specific children into some general comment on the difficulties which many children increasingly experience and the anxieties that they are bound to have which hinder their progress and are of concern to teachers. They may then wonder whether teachers might like to share their experience and to explore with them, in a series of sessions, the range of such pupils in order to find workable solutions for them in classroom situations and may suggest that this might help staff and pupils, as has been shown elsewhere. They would at this stage have to outline what they had in mind, since staff may well expect straight lectures on 'discipline with disruptive pupils', 'the psychology of disturbed children' or 'how to handle children with special needs'. However well-informed and even inspiring such talks may be, most lecturers will have found that, although the audience may find them 'most interesting', some will feel that what has been suggested 'wouldn't work with Tom in my class'. This is exactly the difficulty which a consultative joint problem-solving approach takes account of, and this can be explained when one turns down a request for lectures or other didactic advice.

As outsiders, consultants will increase their credibility if they can give recognition to the difficulties with which teachers have to cope and can show appreciation of the skills with which they tackle them, to which the consultant may be able to make a contribution. In this way the consultant also forestalls being set up as sole expert or his knowledge being perceived as inapplicable to a classroom context. Where a specially qualified member of the staff suggests such joint exploration between professionals with differing expertise, the consultant has to remember that it is the expertise which is different from and additional to their own which teachers expect from him. Pastoral, counselling and special needs support teachers therefore face the particular task of showing that their special skills can support those of their colleagues, without distancing themselves so much from them as to appear unacceptably 'special'. Either way, they will have to deal with questions, many of them unvoiced, in the teachers' minds. (Laslett and Smith (1984) summarise findings with regard to such 'unvoiced questions' as 'will you listen; really listen?', 'does asking for assistance imply incompetence?', 'will you tell the boss?', 'does "help" mean extra work for me?' and 'can anything be done quickly, which will make a difference now?'.) As members of a profession representing authority and 'expected by society [to be] wise, just, capable, competent, knowledgeable' (Taylor 1994), teachers are uneasy about admitting to have difficulties to those who seem to manage or whom they may perceive as critical, as wanting to tell them how to do their job better or as likely to blame them for the children's behaviour. Both internal and external consultants will also have to explain that, while they may well be working directly with some of the pupils in collaboration with classroom teachers, it is not necessary to know the children discussed in their joint explorations or to know them as well as the classroom teacher in daily contact (in contrast with those pupils referred to them directly).

As has been shown, it helps an outside consultant if he can make his offer to the schools of a limited area, such as one or two adjacent neighbourhoods, so that no one set of teachers will feel that they are considered to need special support. Such an offer may be open to any member of staff interested; this is more easily manageable in primary schools but not, as we have seen, impossible at secondary school level. Those who already have pastoral, counselling or tutorial responsibilities may be offered workshops in which they would explore and be helped to develop the skills required to work with teams of colleagues. In either case it is important to recognise and acknowledge the expertise and interests of those with special needs or pastoral responsibilities, who are already likely to be committed to or interested in the idea of consultative support for the staff in general, as complementary to their direct work with pupils.

An offer made on an area basis is likely to lead to requests from some schools for more information. Although such requests usually represent a need, this may be felt only in some parts of the institution. It is therefore crucial to secure the assistance of the head teacher and senior staff by demonstrating (for instance through examples from support work elsewhere) that the aims of such innovative support are congruent with the interests of their school and would, by helping to maximise its professional resources, contribute to the furtherance of its professional goals. Their active support is vital to legitimise the potential group, to protect, as has been stressed, its arrangements against such hazards as simultaneous competing meetings and to allow the growing insights to be put into practice.

A head teacher may also wish to attend the meetings. This will be beneficial for short consultative 'taster' courses under training grant schemes. Where, however, such problem-solving groups are to become an integral part of a school's support network, a Head's regular attendance could easily inhibit the process of skill enhancement by virtue of his position as assessor of staff competence. The consultant will then have to discuss this hazard to obtain the Head's agreement to become an ad hoc attender rather than a regular one. This must be done without appearing to diminish the head teacher's role in providing leadership with regard to the support work. It is crucial that both head teacher and consultant accept the head teacher's lead in defining the work task. Obtaining sanction for the group in this way forestalls a number of difficulties; if the head teacher is present at case discussions before an exploratory climate has been established, teachers may expect him or her to offer solutions before they have themselves examined all the issues underlying the problem – expectations with which the head teacher may unwittingly collude. Nor are all head teachers aware of the effects of their presence among their staff. As Hargreaves (1972) describes, it is very difficult for teachers to talk freely in staff meetings even with head teachers on the best of terms with them. He showed how teachers may try for instance to impersonate what appears to be the head teacher's ideal of a good teacher. However, one can find an equally strong tendency for teachers to refuse to 'put their best foot forward' in the presence of the head teacher and indeed to remain silent in these circumstances. Comments to all these effects were made when the question of inviting their head teachers to join was first raised in developing groups, and some teachers mentioned the risk that they might shape their case presentations and contributions with an eye to the head teacher. There are, then, strong indications that, in the first instance at least, the presence of head teachers or their representatives is likely to inhibit teachers in the task of exploring difficulties experienced with some of their pupils and particularly in discussing any emerging rivalries which are perhaps already dysfunctional for the school. (In my own experience, especially long-term groups do eventually invite their head teachers to attend at later stages, when they have established a way of working. Both teachers and head teachers then found the consultancy mode of working with each other informative and useful, adding a new dimension to cooperation between them.)

It is therefore advisable to remind head teachers who show an interest in the offer of a staff development group how crucial their support of the group will be but how their unavoidable role as assessors of their staff's competence is likely to colour the case presentations should they wish to attend. Most people find it hard to admit problems in their work to their superiors and teachers may thus find it difficult to speak of the matters with which the group should be concerned. Head teachers who had hoped to attend a group from the outset usually then accept that their presence might have an inhibiting effect. This accords with the findings about other consultancy groups (see Daines 1981).

It is also important to discuss with the head teacher the necessity of confidentiality concerning the details of the discussions (the unvoiced question 'will you tell the boss?' listed by Laslett and Smith). This crucial issue can be presented in terms of the obligation imposed on members of any professional group not to discuss outside the group any information gathered there, unless this is clearly in aid of those concerned. This principle admits discretionary discussion between group members and the head teacher – whose sanctioning of the group is thereby also maintained and extended to its potential development into an ongoing support system – and other professionals involved in the child's education and welfare but excludes any references to what individual members have said in the group (and thus takes account of the unvoiced question of whether the boss will be told). (This definition can also help the group later on in their dealings with other professionals, who have been found sometimes to withhold information from teachers out of a misunderstanding of the concept of confidentiality, when having the information might have helped the teacher to meet a child's needs.)

Details such as these constitute important items for the first stage of the negotiations, together with an explanation of the method of consultation and the function of membership (whether, for instance, it is to be open to any member of staff or is to be a group for staff at middle management level, with which some schools may wish to start the development of a staff support and training system). The second stage is then to mention the desirability of an introductory–explanatory meeting with the teaching staff. In some cases, head teachers themselves suggest this; in others, mindful of the likely misconceptions if such a meeting is omitted, the consultant will wish to ask for an opportunity to explain to the teachers what he is offering and to make sure that all understand what such a group would be able to offer and what, together, one may reasonably hope to achieve.

(ii) Introducing consultancy support work to the teaching staff

Once these matters have been clarified, work with the staff can begin with the head teacher's approval. Where a consultant is an outsider, some head teachers, after introducing him to the staff, may remain for the rest of the meeting. One can then, with their agreement, explain in their presence that they would not participate as regular attenders in the proposed group and that proceedings would be confidential. This helps to make it clear from the beginning to both head teacher and staff that one is not to be identified with the interests of either party.

It is useful if this introductory meeting includes, in a primary school, the whole staff if possible, and in a secondary school all the teachers who may be interested in attending a group and as many as want to hear about the work that it may be doing. This is in order to forestall divisions between those who may become members of the pilot group and those who will not. The aim is to set out precisely what it is one is able to offer and what the staff may reasonably hope to gain from it. It is important that as far as possible the whole staff are in touch with the arrangement and are clear about it, to ensure maximum communication, within the framework of confidentiality. If measures aimed at meeting all children's learning needs are to be effective, all their teachers need to be involved.

It helps if one limits oneself to a professionally matter-of-fact terminology and avoids language specific to one's own profession. In addition, such semi-jocular terms as 'worryshop', used by some workers in the field, are best avoided. This has an unhelpful connotation of dilatory inadequacy and risks promoting fantasies about the group and its members. In order to be clear about the group's work, the whole staff requires concise, concrete descriptions of the group's purpose and procedure. They always find it useful to hear of disguised examples of cases discussed in similar groups and how they were dealt with; these should be chosen to illustrate common experiences with children regarded as difficult, the feelings commonly aroused and the alternative ways of dealing with these situations which were worked out.

Everyone must know what contacts there will be between the group members or the consultant and those outside and what their purpose will be. Everyone should feel that the group will not 'cause trouble' or 'want to change everything' but will support the school's educational task and will not antagonise those who do not intend to join. This enables teachers to accept that the head teacher will wish to remain in touch with the group's work and be informed by group members within the confines of confidentiality as outlined.

Divergent interpretations and possible misconceptions still have to be taken into account. If any partisan interests are suspected, defences will be strong. Some may fear to be seen as in need of help by their superiors, while others may have anxieties about an outsider or coordinating colleague, who might judge their performance or omnisciently read their minds – or, even worse, *mis*read them. Yet others may hope for some omnipotence which will bring quick solutions to their difficulties. There will also be different opinions about the proper way to handle classroom difficulties, about whether any but the inexperienced or the inadequate are entitled to have problems and about further typifications of children and parents.

Whether or not such notions are aired, it seems wise to assume their presence. Without explicitly mentioning them, one can start dealing with those unvoiced questions in the course of the discussion, as the main assumptions underlying the consultancy process are spelt out. These relate particularly to problem awareness and commitment to analysing problems and attempting to solve them, as criteria of professionalism. They can be outlined as follows:

(a) that, if problems are articulated while 'hot', in a structured supportive setting, they are likely to be clarified in the process, which may then suggest workable alternative ways of coping with them;

(b) that talking and listening to other professionals may raise our sights as to the possibilities of coping and increase our professional performance;

(c) that through such processes we can learn, without loss of face, when we ourselves unwittingly add to our difficulties;

(d) that such discussions can overcome the conspiracy of silence between colleagues, based on the assumption that teachers ought to have no difficulties and should keep them dark if they do, lest the admission should reflect on their competence – an assumption which is itself detrimental to the professional task;

(e) that, as in other professions, difficulties must be expected at any stage of a career and that the concept of professionalism includes constructive analysis of the reasons for any problem, so that it may be resolved;

(f) that this may also release our professional creativeness, tap unexpected resources within ourselves and enhance the support which professionals can give each other.

One can then briefly describe the structure of the sessions as, for instance, a sequence of:

1. Case presentations, in each of which a teacher very briefly outlines a child's behaviour in school, the solutions attempted and their results as he perceives them.

2. Gathering of additional information:

(a) through questions from the group about any further details which they might think relevant;

(b) by contributions from those group members who know the child or his family and may know details unknown to the presenter since their contact has been in other classes, different departments of the school or other schools which the child or his siblings have attended: this additional information, being pooled, may well reveal additional factors contributing to the difficulty.

3. Joint exploration of issues on the basis of all the information now available, including its implications for alternative approaches to the child, his parents, the whole class and the learning task. Such discussion is directed to finding educational means to modify and extend the child's experience.

This allows one to show how joint exploration and pooled experience enable the presenter of a case to take a fresh look at the situation and to decide for himself how to employ his skills in the light of increased understanding. It also demonstrates how each case explored in this way involves every member of the group, whether or not the child is known to others present, and shows how this can help them all to build up a framework for analysing and approaching other problems as they arise. With this objective established, there is little danger of teachers losing interest during the discussion of each other's cases, as happened in some of the groups observed by Daines and her team (1981). Evaluation of results from the groups of two sample years referred to earlier has shown that the teachers did indeed find the exploration of their colleagues' cases – regardless of a pupil's age – as useful as that of their own.

At this stage of the negotiations, possibilities can be shown, misconceptions and false hopes can be dealt with and a base of receptivity be created both for the proposed group to proceed from and for the interest of its non-member colleagues. As one tries to convey one's understanding of the teachers' work, setting and appreciation of their responsibilities and constraints, it is possible and crucial to show one's own expertise as supportive of theirs but also to seek to make alternatives thinkable.

Before the staff decide whether they wish to start a consultancy support group, one needs to make sure that the ground rules and obligations arising from membership are established to forestall those difficulties already referred to. It is important here to give some guidance on optimum arrangements for the size of group, the range and function of membership, the length of the pilot course, of individuals' attendance during a course, the timing of sessions and the length of meetings. It helps if this guidance is seen to be based on experience with other groups of teachers – the consultant's own or that of others as more evidence becomes now available – in different settings.

As to *size*, on short 'taster' courses or single in-service days one may have to work with the whole staff of a school, after an introductory talk. 'Fishbowl' arrangements (an inner circle working group, with an outer circle monitoring the process, changing over at half-time) can then accommodate numbers as large as the staff of a comprehensive school. For groups to develop as an integral part of the staff's whole-school approach, however, it seems that groups of up to 12 members (some of them core members, others with short-term commitments, as outlined below) offer maximum benefit of members' range of experience and expertise. Larger groups are known to hinder frank expression of ideas when perceived or projected feelings of the group may influence or prevent contributions. A larger group would also mean that the presenter of a case would be bombarded with more contributions from fellow members than he could examine; and the consultant might have to deflect an unmanageable number of anecdotes or assertive statements – to help the group stay with the case – and some members might become silent passengers. It would then be difficult for the consultant not to act like a chairman or seminar tutor on whom the group would be ambivalently dependent. This would interfere with the coordinate interdependence essential to the process of joint exploration.

As to *membership*, one can outline the advantage of heterogeneous groups, which may contain members from the network of schools serving one community or, if confined to one school, from the range of departments and career experience. In accordance with Eggleston's (1977) analysis of the influence of individual perception and interpretation on a school's 'ecosystem', consultancy group membership will be significant both as regards the *number* of people who will be reached as the group develops and grows into an ongoing support system and as regards the *range* of positions and responsibilities which they hold. Schools will differ in their decisions whether this should best start with a group open to staff regardless of status and length of career experience or with a training group for staff with special responsibilities who then assist in the development of support groups across the school. All teachers are, of course, as 'grass-roots care-takers' (Caplan 1961) key people, because of their psychological significance for children, parents and colleagues. Caplan also stressed the importance of affecting a significant proportion of the forces which influence individual and institutional emotional health and have implications for both administrative action and personal interaction. The effect of a support system on the institution as a whole will depend on the number and positions of those members of the hierarchy who have, by attending, developed their perception of their responsibilities with regard to children's special needs and the way in which they exercise them, both with individual children and with features of the institution which they discover to be detrimental to its primary task of education.

Depending on the length of course envisaged for the pilot group, the self-selection of members may be on both core and short-term bases, which increases the proportion of staff who can become actively involved. For instance, a two-school group, limited to 12 attenders at any one time, with four core members attending for a year and with planned turnover of eight short-term members at the end of each term, would be able to involve 28 teachers from both schools. This would incorporate as many teachers as the staff of many junior schools, and more than the staff of many infant schools. A four-school group, with eight core members and planned turnover of four short-term members at each half-term and end of term, can accommodate the same number of teachers for twice as many schools. These were the working arrangements of the group whose case discussions are described on pages 27–34. I have also found that a much smaller proportion of the teachers in a large school can form a significant bridge between members and non-members, provided that they have – or are helped to have, through the group's focus on interaction skills – active contact with their colleagues across the departments. At the comprehensive school with a staff of over 80 whose case discussions were described on pages 41 to 48, 12 teachers representing a good range of experience and subjects, at first volunteered to compose a group for one term, with the option of a second term and some staff change-over if desired. The option was taken up during the second half of the first term. Eight members of the group wished to stay with it for this second term, and four new members could be admitted. The 16 people thus involved decided at the final evaluation meeting to organise a continuing staff support group, without external help, for the following year. This appears to have been successful, according to the comments of such independent witnesses as the staff of the child guidance clinic in touch with the school, and even led to the formation of an additional parallel group. The scope for a single group is remarkably wide – especially if one considers the relatively small amount of time for which any one consultant may be made available in any particular school or area.

The advantages of heterogeneous groups, with regard both to range of experience and information about the pupil discussed and to range of members' expertise, may have become obvious when the structure of the sessions was discussed. However, these concern also the teachers as colleagues. Younger teachers have commented on the reassurance that they derived from hearing their seniors admitting difficulties regardless of length of experience, while older ones welcomed the infectious strengths of recent commitment to the educational enterprise and its challenges and also the reminder of the need of the inexperienced for their support. It helps to stress these features at this stage, both to deal with the unvoiced questions regarding the equation of having difficulties with assumed incompetence and in anticipation of the likelihood of needing to deal constructively with questions of status and length of experience once the group has started (see page 125) .

The length of the course envisaged for the pilot group will affect arrangements for membership. For some groups, teachers are able to decide on a two- or three-term contract with core members attending throughout and carefully planned short-term membership with turnover each half-term. Colleagues with additional knowledge of a pupil whose case is to be discussed, or colleagues dealing with sudden crisis cases, can be invited to attend ad hoc. To other groups, it may be possible to offer one-term contracts, with or without option for a further term. The most obvious advantage of long-term groups is that they are able to follow up cases and to examine how the children's needs evolve. They can thereby further reduce the ever-present hazard of 'confirming' children's difficulties through initial diagnoses based on a confusion of symptoms with explanations – or of defining the whole pupil in terms of the initial diagnosis of deviance.

Even short-term pilot groups, however, can show teachers that workable alternatives may be found for many situations which they had deemed beyond their scope (for example the group described in Teresa's case). Interestingly, in my study of ten different school settings in the two sample years already referred to, teachers who attended a one-year group for five weeks were more emphatic about their gains from attending than were those who attended seven sessions for one term in a group which ended with that term. This, of course, raises the issue of reinforcement from within the institution. The fact that short-term members of a long-term group could remain in contact throughout (they could for instance return for follow-ups and evaluation meetings and generally followed developments with great interest), also promoted more easily a climate of consultative support in the whole institution.

It is possible at this stage to mention to teachers interested in a pilot support arrangement of at least two terms, of core and short-term members, that these roles are to be seen as complementary (rather than just a matter of individual preference). For instance, new short-term members offer constant reminders of the range of problems and their reiteration in an ever-new guise, and core members give groups the necessary continuity. Core members also have the most continuous opportunity of developing those support skills which may enable them to consolidate a staff development system in their school. There was also evidence that they used these skills more effectively with other groups, such as feeder schools, pupils' families and other services in the welfare network. This kind of staff development thus also points to ways of overcoming the at times conflicting perceptions and interventions of disparate services (see Jeanie's case, pp. 34–41, and Chapter 7).

A group structure which balances continuity with change of membership in this way is also able to cater for the frustrations of fluctuating membership reported by Daines (1981). It can do so quite purposefully as it also offers an opportunity to examine the implications for teachers of such changes in group membership, since similar changes constantly affect their classrooms and the school as a whole. A pupil who has been absent has to rejoin a group whose recent experiences he has not shared; new pupils, and teachers, join and others leave, and rarely is sufficient account taken of the feelings of apprehension and loss thus generated. Since most of us at least appear to take such changes in our stride, teachers can be unaware of how children's past experiences may make them vulnerable to such situations. Unaware of the sense of abandonment which children may feel, teachers about to leave often think it best not to tell the children until their day of departure and thus leave the children to cope on their own with the range of conflicting emotions which that entails. There are as yet few schools which require the idea of sufficient 'notice' to include the children, to work with them through these experiences of loss and transition and to give them hope for new learning because the good of the past experience will not be obliterated in their own and the teacher's mind. References to this aspect of children's needs in the life of the school and their school life occur naturally where it is also part of the life of the group.

More schools are now trying to bridge the transition from one school to another, at least academically through meetings of staff teaching certain subjects. The consultation groups have found, however, that meaningful communication between schools about children's individual needs (i.e. more than forwarding records about them) is equally important and valuable. A school needs to know which of its new pupils have been receiving special attention at the school that they are leaving and what approaches have been found to answer best with each child. Scharff and Hill (1976) make similar points about school leavers 'between two worlds' and make a case for anticipatory guidance during the last year at school and a curriculum which takes account of the heightened apprehensions, anxieties and needs at this time of transition. However, they also found that, because of the exceptional organisational pressures in secondary schools at the end of the academic year, teachers are often least available to their pupils just when they are needed most.

Teachers themselves, of course, may remember the 'de-skilling shock experiences' with which newcomers to the teaching profession may be greeted by their more experienced colleagues and the lack of any usable support. As such experiences have ripple effects in the classroom, it is clearly valuable to examine the underlying issues. As has been shown, the reception of newcomers can affect their self-concept and a critical reception maintains the closure of the group to outside influences. Support groups which combine long-term and short-term membership naturally bring such issues to attention, as change itself becomes part of the structure designed to meet its members' immediate and long-term professional needs.

As to *timing and length of meetings*, conflicts with the school timetable need of course to be forestalled if the group is not to feel constantly rushed. This can be done best if the consultant can offer a choice between one and one and a quarter hours during lunchtime – provided that teachers are freed from competing commitments – and between one and a quarter and one and a half hours at the end of the school day. With this choice, teachers tend to prefer the later time, when there are fewer distractions. More can also be achieved in the longer meeting, which teachers appreciate. Yet both alternatives have worked well in different schools. Whatever the arrangement, however, it is crucial to stress the importance of regular attendance for a stretch of time and of agreeing on starting and finishing times which every attender can manage. Latecomers would miss the case presentation with which the meeting begins and could therefore not contribute meaningfully or gain much from the discussion, while early leavers would forego the accumulative effect of the discipline and content of joint explorations.

Consultants to a pilot group are likely to find, at least initially, weekly meetings an ideal arrangement, ten sessions per term from the second week of term to about the last but one. It seems a good idea to preserve maximum continuity while allowing for the additional demands made on teachers at the beginning and end of term. Furthermore, unfinished business which is bound to remain at the end of meetings has a way of 'working itself through' between weekly sessions, can throw new light on the previous week's deliberations and facilitates the development of a framework for the analysis of problems in general. With longer spaces in between, the sheer quantity of disparate happenings and demands which fill even a fortnight of school life can easily obliterate such connections or detract from their relevance.

If there is a virtue in accepting the unavoidability of loose ends at the conclusion of meetings, it would clearly be unwise to leave too many to the space between meetings. This could be a risk in this kind of work if one were to follow the pattern of most external in-service courses, with their two-hour meetings. Teachers readily accept a time limit of one and a quarter or one and a half hours if one points out that one may 'get lost in cases' if too much time is given to their exploration. Also, an additional half hour at the end of a busy day may make all the difference between feeling recharged by sharing experiences and being overtaxed by the intensity of the activity. The time limit may also help members to accept that loose ends will have to be lived with.

When matters such as these are raised in the introductory meeting – by which time a sufficient number of teachers may well be wishing to attend such a group in their school – there are usually questions on what preparation a case presentation requires (see the unvoiced question of 'does it mean extra work for me?'). In our case there was no preparation necessary apart from verbal presentation of the cases' most salient features (see p. 118). Questions also arise on the number of cases that one might deal with in any one session. In consultancy sessions with doctors, Gosling (1965) indicates a preference for two cases rather than one per session, but consultants to teachers will differ on what structure they feel their meetings require. When discussing the case of a pupil, teachers need to consider a wide range of information, including the pupil's relationships with other teachers, with school mates and in the family. Gathering this information in the meeting and discussing its implications takes more time at first but speeds up as members observe the relevance and significance of information pooled and gear their questions accordingly. Thus a group at the beginning may need to devote a whole session to each case, but after a while may be able to consider two per session or to include one or two follow-ups. Limiting the initial presentation of detail to its most salient features also prevents overwhelming the group by more detail than they are at first able to handle but ensures sufficient time for thoughtful discussion. Attention to the relevance of every discussion to problems in general will reassure those who were envisaging a greater number of cases per session.

Having clarified these considerations during the introductory session – more briefly than had to be done in these pages – staff will then want some time to consider their implications for them, before work can begin with the prospective group members.

Work with the groups

(i) Early group meetings: fixed roles, hierarchies and expectations about the consultant's role

The consultancy model here adopted is based, as was outlined, on the principle of joint exploration within a setting of coordinate relationships. However, such relationships cannot be assumed to exist at the outset. Many teachers will find it difficult at first to adjust to this kind of participation, may try to assume fixed roles – from 'resident cynic' to 'rebel' and 'realist' – and there will be many attempts to perpetuate a hierarchy. Consultants will know that it is easier to handle such attempts sooner rather than later and may have begun to forestall them already in the introductory meeting.

Where the support group contains a wide range of career experience, there may easily be deliberate or unwitting attempts to reproduce the institution's hierarchy in the group. Holders of senior appointments may, for instance, rightly or wrongly feel that their younger colleagues expect from them ready answers or, as happened in one group, may try to influence the selection of pupils for discussion. Their authority may be deferred to or resisted by less senior colleagues. Either way this will hinder a genuine exploration of issues and of their implications for the individual teacher. A consultant will try to forestall such situations but may have to handle them as they arise (see Vic's case, pp. 32–5) on how the issue of hierarchy conflict could be used on behalf of both child and staff, without loss of face). Where the essential features of procedure were established in the introductory meeting, members can now just be reminded, without embarrassment to either side, that each teacher needs to select his or her own case, that there should be no interruption of the presentation and that eliciting further detail *follows* the presentation so that everybody is able to look at the whole situation and nobody suggests solutions before all available information has been examined. As the exploration proceeds, one can then turn contributions, made from seemingly superior or inferior stances or from fixed role positions, into additional knowledge which illuminates the case, irrespective of the status of the contributor, his length of experience, or the role that he has chosen to assume (see the discussion of Dave, pp. 35–8), showing how his teacher was helped unobtrusively to relinquish his fixed role). What Caplan calls 'the authority of ideas', rather than status, can then do its work, confirming for members of both high and low status the relevance and complementary nature of their experience. It helps if all of us, no matter how many pupils we have taught or treated, remember that we need to look afresh at each new case – similar to expert musicians whose playing will suffer to the extent to which it suggests merely a repeat performance.

With all expertise thus shared in the joint effort of fresh exploration, the problem can be returned to the presenting teacher, who is now left to approach it anew, assured by the support experienced and the confidence conveyed that a fresh start is possible. It should be no surprise that even first appointments respond to being treated as autonomous authentic professionals and as part of a network of relationships across the whole hierarchy, which can support the competence of every member.

Dealing with expectations about a consultant's role

Expectations exist from the moment that an offer of support has been made and will be influenced by teachers' attitudes to 'support', by their work setting and, as we saw, by the way in which the offer reaches them. Groups may expect the consultant to assume a leadership role beyond the exigencies of the first meetings. The consultant is certainly responsible for ensuring the observance of the exploratory sequence. He has to ensure that issues are highlighted, that focus remains on the task and that participation does not become judgemental but remains supportive. All this demands a temporarily high profile which members may expect to continue. Group members' unrealistic expectations of instant solutions may further be reinforced in the honeymoon period by seemingly miraculous changes in pupil behaviour which are attributed to the consultant's knowledge.

Collusion with any such false ideas would clearly be detrimental to the objectives of this form of consultancy – the achievement of autonomy in understanding behaviour and working out the implications for action. Any such collusion would also interfere with the consultant's own sensitivity to how the case and the situation presented are being received by the group. For the group, this can only lead to disappointment. It is therefore crucial from the very first case exploration to stress that none of us knows the answers at this stage but that together we can collect further information which may help us to clarify the issues. If one can show appreciation of the teacher's difficulties as natural and understandable, convey confidence in the group members as professionals with their own expertise and show one's own courage not to know as a vantage point from which to proceed, it will be easier for the members to accept more realistically what expertise one has to contribute as being neither omniscient nor disappointingly useless, in exactly the way in which one accepts their contributions.

In this way, one can ensure that no member has to bear the brunt of criticism or becomes the target of unsubstantiated ideas for solutions implying judgement of his way of handling the case. One can take care that seemingly outrageous features of a situation do not swallow all attention, by inviting members to consider the less obvious aspects of the case, to find their interrelation and possible significance. One may have to check over-talkative members tactfully by inviting contributions, early and unobtrusively, from anyone who is tempted to carry the role of silent member. This attempt to forestall the kind of role fix which may hinder individuals from deriving maximum professional gain can also assist in helping teachers to appreciate the importance of avoiding role fixing in their classrooms (discussed on p. 60), when their efforts with individual children are so often blocked by classroom groups who fix them in a group role detrimental to their development.

Since the teachers are to find their own informed way towards workable solutions, the consultancy support group needs to contain from the start an unobtrusive element of training in that direction. This will include paying attention to the special skills of attentiveness – Reik's (1947) 'listening with the third ear' – which is crucial to the understanding of individual needs as encountered in the classroom and between colleagues, in furtherance of the professional task. For this reason, too, it is advisable to discourage the reading out of prepared accounts of cases, which would obscure the teacher's feelings about particular features and tends to make listening more difficult. Written notes just for reference, to aid presentation and exploration, can be very useful, however, and deserve support. In this context, one can also explain at the very beginning features of one's own way of working which may be misinterpreted, for instance where the consultant himself prefers to make brief notes during the presentation of its main points, for reference during the exploration and for later follow-ups. Such notes will also allow him, at later meetings, to help a group to become aware of its achievements.

Groups sometimes expect the consultant, at the end of a first meeting, to summarise the main points of a case. To do so may not always be appropriate. It would for instance run counter to the aims of consultancy as outlined, if such summary were to offer only one person's opinion as to which points are essential, and would suggest a leader's assumption of consensus about a case which will need much further thought by everybody. However, it may be useful periodically to highlight, by summarising, the essentials of the *process* and *sequence* of exploring a case at the end of a discussion (such as how the group looked at a child's actual behaviour, tried to see it in the context of what was known about him and so on, as outlined on p. 51), which can assist in developing the problem approach skills which teachers need to apply when faced with pupils' difficulties in the classroom.

On account of the need for further thought about the issues highlighted, there is also in these meetings no 'final' decision-making stage which teachers may at first expect. As the case remains the responsibility of the teacher who presented it, it is that teacher who now has to use what better understanding resulted from the session and to work out the implications for himself. This process is helped if one sees that each meeting finishes on a positive note. In the same way, one may have to reinforce the importance of this when teachers finish a lesson, dismiss children at the end of the day or conclude a meeting with parents (the parallels between consultancy and teaching skills have already been referred to elsewhere in this book). The case explorations illustrated in Part I show how these processes may develop at the different stages of a group's life.

(ii) Stages of development in the groups

The detailed accounts of the case discussions given earlier are naturally much abbreviated descriptions of what happened in any one session. With each case, teachers are encouraged both to follow a systematic course of joint exploration of the details reported (such as outlined on p. 57) and then to 'follow the material where it leads'. This way of working often calls for a considerable change of attitude and the development of skills which they may not so far have practised. Outsiders to the groups, or intermittent attenders such as head teachers, often noticed these changes, and participants themselves commented on them. They may for instance be reflected in a new degree of confidence and competence in presentation and discussion in general which members may demonstrate in the course of time. We have already seen that there can be a number of obstacles which may impede a group's progress. However, where these have been satisfactorily negotiated, a pattern of development emerges, which in template form, and at the risk of oversimplification which ignores individual differences, may be described as follows.

The consultant may find that, during early sessions, cases tend to be presented haltingly and cautiously and that the consultant himself has to elicit essential facts by a few questions and promptings. Children tend to be described in generalities, often without concrete detail ('a worrier', 'can't do anything on his own', 'always in trouble', 'a thorough nuisance' or 'an aggressive child'). Behaviour may be mentioned without reference to the child's probable feelings, while the teacher's own feelings may colour the presentation. The problem tends to be seen as 'out there', in the pupil, his home circumstances or the school system, or the teacher may blame himself in anticipation of expected judgements. The teacher may hope for or expect explicit advice on what to do but may also be ambivalent about the expected instructions and may accept with some relief the encouragement to use his or her own judgement on the basis of the issues highlighted. The consultant has to ensure that the group looks at these, stays with the case or comes back to it, examines the issues before formulating answers and considers assumptions about a child's behaviour without implying criticism of those who hold them. He must watch that the discussion encourages teachers to look at the implications and cease to see descriptions ('just an attention-seeker') as explanations. Teachers may be staggered by the improvements in the pupils' behaviour which may follow their first attempts to try the ideas aired. The consultant must watch that he does not allow these changes to be attributed to his expertise since this would imply that improvements are the results of techniques which have been taught rather than of growth in understanding, must watch that such dramatic changes are not mistaken for permanent solutions to a difficulty, and that they are not expected in each case. In addition, it is important that their non-appearance is not seen as a reflection on the teacher's skill.

As the course develops, teachers will take note of the consultant's systematic interest in the antecedents of the incidents mentioned and in the child's reactions to those of the teacher and other children. They themselves include more and more objective details in their presentation of a case and refer more often to how the child may be experiencing the situation. This enables the consultant to assume a lower profile during the information gathering stage, intervening mainly at the later stages to ensure the fullest possible examination of issues and implications. The teachers can admit uncertainties more readily, show enjoyment of their extending resourcefulness and describe how their attitudes to difficult pupils have changed and how their relationships with them improve. Such improvements are increasingly attributed to changes in their own awareness and to having shared a problem objectively. They can begin to 'ignore' the consultant in the face of their own acknowledged expertise. Encouraged to examine a child's whole situation and how teachers are involved in it, they more readily include themselves as part of it. They accept that, even with back-up consultation, problems will hardly ever go away overnight and that needs will evolve and require further observation and management. Also, they may generally admit that their own exploration of the issues involved is more valuable than merely receiving advice.

Skills may be used with increasing sensitivity, in relation to both child and parent. We saw how in Michael's case (pp. 30–32), the teachers talked about the respect owed to complex relationships and the importance of not pushing advice with parents, in line with their own experience of the consultant's similar approach to them. It is also of interest to note how newcomers to a group are able to benefit from joining it at this later stage and from its earlier explorations, their awareness and actions reflecting the stage reached by the group as a whole. Short-term members, too, are helped by the questions that others have learned to ask themselves and to negotiate the earlier stages of the core group more rapidly.

Eventually, presentations and explorations become shorter and more concise, as more shared understanding has emerged from past joint discussions. This makes it easier to consider two cases in one session. More teachers now give clear indications that they have already been using their extended skills with the new case which they are presenting, including these in the presentation. This, too, can apply even to new short-term members who joined the groups later but had followed their development through discussions with colleagues, before joining – a sign that members and non-attending colleagues were clearly helping each other. Group members referred to this spontaneously and consistently at follow-up meetings as long as one and two years after a pilot course.

(iii) Case follow-ups

When one mentions in the introductory meeting that case follow-ups will be an integral part of the work, teachers are usually particularly interested, as they can bring anything that they try out back into the group for evaluation, instead of being left to get on with it. This opportunity is clearly desirable and easier to offer where meetings follow a weekly pattern. The longer the interval between sessions, the more difficult this will be, as teachers will then tend to crowd each new meeting with ever-new cases.

A case follow-up provides the chance to take account of how children's needs evolve after their case has been presented and their situation explored and what further skills and awareness this requires from teachers. It means that teachers can be further assisted to develop the kind of climate in which they continue to learn from the child. Difficulties in ordinary schools are frequently aggravated by teachers unwittingly defining their pupils in terms of their own first spontaneous reaction to overt behaviour and by then behaving towards them in ways which reproduce the unacceptable behaviour that they are trying and have managed momentarily to correct (such as praising a child for improvement by contrasting it with his former behaviour, to which he then reverts – 'thank goodness, a good piece of writing at last! but why did it have to take so long?' – reminding the child, as Stott (1982) remarks, 'that he is forgetting his resolve to be bloody-minded').

When cases are followed up over a period of time, skills and techniques can be developed to counter ingrained habits such as these. Less faith is placed in dramatic improvements, and there is less disappointment when these improvements are not maintained and behaviour deteriorates. Temporary deteriorations can be appreciated for instance as the child's way of testing the teacher's changed attitude or as re-enacting behaviour patterns established from the past and too deeply ingrained to be overcome in a short time.

The intention to focus the teachers' attention on evolving needs has implications for the handling of follow-ups. Early in a group's life, some teachers may hesitate to offer a follow-up, especially if they have nothing spectacular to report when others are delightedly talking about miraculous improvements. Tempting as it may be for the consultant to share this delight or to praise the teacher for such improvement, one should make it clear that improvement will not always follow and that it is not the teacher's performance which will be evaluated but the child's needs and response to what has been attempted. In distinction to behavioural consultancy the Caplan model avoids praising group members' good results, as this would imply disappointment with a less good result as a reflection on the teacher.

To underline these points, and to lessen any sense of being checked for delivery of goods, it seems best to leave the timing of follow-ups to the teacher, emphasising the needs of the case. Instead of questioning teachers, as one might do as a supervisor, one can temporarily close a case, unanxiously suggesting that it be considered again when more is known. The group's genuine interest in how a case develops after their initial exploration, and the consultant's confidence in the teacher's ability to work out the implications and to re-examine the situation, are usually sufficient to bring a follow-up, without reducing the teacher's sense of autonomy.

It is also useful to remind teachers that 'cure' (with its unfortunate connotation of completion at a fixed point) is neither our aim nor within our scope but that 'care' and 'response-ability' can release children's powers of self-repair and so promote growth and improvement (both 'cure' and 'care' having been conjoint qualities of the original concept of the Latin cura, now preserved only in modern language derivatives (e.g. curator, curé, Kur)). Teachers thus come to share with the consultant both knowledge and skills related to each case from the first presentation to follow-up. As we saw, teachers were found to consider follow-up of their colleagues' cases, despite their not knowing the children, as useful as that of their own. If this is not the experience of all consultants (Daines 1981) or one's own experience in every group, it suggests important implications for the structure of group sessions. It raises the issue of the use made of experience in the group, to aid evolving skills and self-awareness irrespective of which case is being followed through.

(iv) Interpretations and interim evaluations

'Interpreting' experiences in the group

As we saw in Part I, aspects of a case presented may be reflected in the group itself as it discusses the child's situation. In some instances, it may be appropriate not to attempt to interpret – but to comment on this, specifically or in general terms at group level, without infringement of the principle of consultancy as personally non-intrusive (since consultancy groups are not first and foremost self-awareness groups where members gather explicitly for that purpose).

Teachers who complain about their pupils' unpunctuality may, for instance, present the group with this problem by arriving late for meetings when they could have avoided this. One group had been preoccupied with the difficulty of getting homework from certain children. They themselves had been asked to answer a questionnaire for the purpose of evaluating their experience in the support group, but several members failed to return it. With some lightness of touch such parallels can be pointed out, and the teachers may be able to examine their reasons for their own failure to meet agreed requests; this may illuminate the failure of the children and the extent to which the teachers may be supporting the behaviour which they think they are discouraging.

A group which is usually lively may become withdrawn when a withdrawn child is under consideration whose problem they may feel unable to explore. Similarly, groups may become hyperactive in discussing a 'hyperactive' child. The presenting teacher may be 'all over the place' in his description, and teacher and group may seem to set each other off with the same reciprocal effect as that between child and teacher. One teacher described how a pair of unruly twins drove her to distraction with their inability to stick to demands that she made. To the amazement of the group a colleague of hers, trying to elaborate her presentation of the twins, did so in such a way that it became difficult for the group to keep track of the case, having to deal with 'unruly twins' in the group itself. Such parallels are easy and useful to discuss and do not create counter-productive defensive resistance which statements can call forth from a seemingly omniscient interpreter.

Other parallels may be less obvious. In Dipak's case (pp. 45–8) the teachers had complained that their superiors would not listen to them and that this made them feel frustrated and hopeless. None of them noticed how similar this was to their response to Dipak. Once this was aired, they could appreciate the hopelessness which their response to the boy's irritating behaviour might itself have been generating. They could then explore patterns of authority and dependence between pupils and teachers and between teachers in the staff hierarchy. They could also consider why they found the boy's behaviour so irritating and how certain ways of demanding advice and help invited refusal from senior colleagues – and in this case the consultant. This made it possible to explore how such behaviour increased mutual frustration.

In Tony's case (pp. 19–24), the teacher became suddenly aware, as she was describing it, that she was responding to the child's crisis like the family, hectically keeping everybody busy in order to escape dealing with the problem. In contrast, the case of Dave and his teacher (pp. 35–8) illustrates the potential of delayed comment on the whole experience in retrospect.

The *timing of comments* is clearly important and requires careful judgement. It will depend both on the effect which the group's behaviour is having on the case exploration and on the effect which the comment is likely to have on the discussion; withdrawn behaviour (failure to discuss) or hyperactivity (disjointed jumping from one point to another) are clearly not conducive to greater understanding. In both cases the parallels with the child's problems were pointed out, and this facilitated purposeful discussion. However, with Dave's teacher it was better not to comment while he was feeling helpless but to do so later, when things had improved and the experience could be considered as a whole. To make these comments earlier would probably have added to his despondency and have increased his resistance to altering his perception of Dave. In Vic's case (pp. 32–5) we had both immediate and postponed comments. A fleeting reference to the way in which the head teacher and probationary teacher seemed at times to re-enact the kind of relationship which distressed the child at home and thus provoked a parallel response in the child was part of the discussion of a phenomenon known in other professions as well. This intrigued them and enabled them – without loss of face or need to climb down – to work more harmoniously together.

If such comments on analogies between the group's behaviour and that of the child under discussion are timed acceptably, they can, as we saw, lead to further understanding of the child's problems. To consolidate such insights for professional use, however, may require greater detachment, such as can develop in spontaneous and planned interim evaluations.

Interim evaluations

Opportunities for evaluation and consolidation of insight may occur spontaneously during particularly 'good' or 'bad' meetings. They may also be planned for set times, such as mid-term and the end of term, as an integral part of the course of group meetings, to consider the effect of work in the group on the professional task. Again, as has been stressed, in contrast with some other forms of group work such as psychotherapy or counselling, there is in professional consultation no mandate for exploration of personal matters. Evaluation of any growth in self-awareness and its significance for the professional task must therefore not involve any intrusion into members' personal concerns.

Spontaneous evaluations pertain to phases and stages of development as a group may experience them. In our case these will to some extent be affected also by the stresses and strains of the school year, and there will be periods when it is appropriate to note how both previous experiences in the group and events in the school may be affecting the mood of the meeting. A group is likely to begin with high expectations and go through courtship and honeymoon phases, intensified by improvements in pupils' behaviour which may seem dramatic results of the work in the group. As such initial improvements are unlikely to be maintained; disappointment will follow as long as teachers expect a panacea for success and while they overrate success and undervalue the educative potential of disillusion and failure. The task of the consultant is then to make the group face this paradox, that periods of disappointment and depression can be valuable by making us think and promoting new capacity for concern and a renewed search for understanding (in the affective as well as the cognitive sense), both personally and professionally.

During such periods it is useful to point out to a group that one is not attempting to remove their depression or disappointment but to see whether one can find through it new capacities for understanding and toleration which may enable them to help children to cope with theirs. Such evaluative comments may themselves help a group to move forwards, quite suddenly at times. It was in one such 'depressed' session, for instance, that Michael's teacher (pp. 30–32) reported his improvement, following her earlier failure with him. This almost electrified the group into seeing both failure and success as part of a process, facilitated in the non-judgemental climate of consultation which neither overrates success nor undervalues failure. Teachers found that reflection on such phases in the group could also help them with their discouraged pupils.

At interim evaluations planned in advance for a set time, the groups will spontaneously bring up points as they occur to them. The points which come up this way, without prompting, will be the best indicators of how effective the support has been for its members. Such evaluations tend to have a developmental pattern of their own.

At the first of such evaluations, members tend to be concerned with what they feel to be of benefit to themselves as teachers. Having come to obtain practical advice for a specific case, they may say that they are now more likely to think things through instead, learning to be their own best advisers. Both the teachers' and the head teachers' groups attributed this to the effect of sharing their concerns in a situation structured to deal with them (in contrast, for instance, to staffroom moans about difficult pupils). This kind of *sharing*, they felt, helped them:

- to *distance* themselves from the difficulty as they tried to describe it to supportive colleagues;
- to *recognise* their own situation in that of others;
- to *refocus* their attention in the processes of questioning and examining, noticing how their own changing awareness then affected their relationship with the pupil in such a way that he could change his behaviour in turn.

Later evaluations tend to show a shift in emphasis, from being more aware of their *own* perceptions of others and the effect of their expectations on them to an awareness of what *others*, rightly or wrongly, might be expecting of the teachers and how such expectations affected both sides. During their discussions they had come to experience – rather than theorise about – the need to understand what either side may be attributing to the other, as a precondition for meaningful communication. During evaluation periods such insights seemed to be consolidated, cognitively as well as affectively.

The essential aim of such evaluation meetings is to help teachers not only to feel more hopeful about coping with difficulties but also to substantiate this feeling. Such confirmation is essential if 'understanding the other side' is to bear fruit with their pupils and with those whose support they need to enlist on the pupils' behalf, such as parents, colleagues or other professionals and officials in a position to affect a child's education and welfare (see Chapters 6 and 7).

(v) Endings and post-course follow-ups

There may be no 'endings' where a member of staff has succeeded in developing an ongoing support system. Where the arrangement is a pilot course initiated and run by an outsider to the school, post-course follow-ups, in addition to evaluations and follow-up sessions during the course, will be important. Such follow-ups can help to preserve what has been learnt on the course as well as to facilitate further developments which may lead to an ongoing resource and support system. This then raises a number of issues, first of all that of when and how to end a course and contact with a group, to aid such development.

A collaborative problem-solving programme concerned with the acquisition of skills and the development of understanding in the field of special emotional and social needs is likely to assume particular personal significance for its members, enabling them to incorporate whatever they come to feel as of special significance to themselves, as insight into such needs and appropriate responses to them is built up. Throughout the course, there will have been ambivalent feelings about such learning, resolved to varying degrees in the process of exploration. Depending on how far they were resolved, participants in a course which links professional understanding and competence with self-awareness may for this very reason wish the contact to continue beyond the point of actual professional need (just as, conversely, others may leave the course prematurely before accepting the interconnection).

Towards the end of a course, earlier uncertainties may be reactivated, and members may again give the consultant all the credit for their improved competence and potential for change and hold him responsible for everything that they have learnt. Aspects of endings and transitions will have been examined in case discussions when pupils or teachers leave, and prospects such as return visits may be used to mitigate fears about separation. Now, endings and future contacts are aspects to deal with in the groups themselves. (A sensitive account of what beginnings and endings of a course of study may mean to pupils and teachers can be found in the book by Salzberger-Wittenberg *et al.* (1983).)

For reasons such as these, endings have to be prepared weeks ahead. This can be done by mentioning in good time the possibility of having follow-up sessions and trying to clarify their purpose, so that they do not become just a device for postponing the ending. Their aims might be to review the course and what longer-term effects it may turn out to have, to deepen understanding and to strengthen skills developed during it and since, or to assist in extending the climate of consultancy in the school through staff development groups of their own.

The first post-course follow-up meeting needs to be timed well, neither too soon nor too late; an interval of a term or so seems a good time. In one case, for various reasons, the first follow-up did not occur until a year after termination. The discussion demonstrated that members, while they seemed to have maintained the level of insight and practice achieved on the course (this was the group which contained Don's, Michael's and Vic's teachers), had felt abandoned. Better-timed follow-up with other groups led at first to intermittent contact with the consultant and then to a 'continuing conference', to which any member of staff could bring cases for joint exploration. After a year of such intermittent meetings (the consultant attending their regular meetings only once or twice a term), one may find that staff and head teacher have themselves become consultants to each other. This will be a good point at which to leave the staff to their own conference.

Some groups do not suggest that they would like to have a follow-up meeting (as was the case with the group who had discussed Teresa). Although it is preferable for contact to be continued by request, the consultant can also suggest a further meeting, as was done there for six months later, since their course had only lasted one term, had amounted to seven sessions because of several unavoidable interruptions and had ended rather uneasily. In this case, the interest thus manifested by suggesting a further meeting helped to relieve the group's mixed feelings. Wanting to find out after this interval what the teachers felt that they had been able to learn from an unduly curtailed course proved the consultant's genuine interest and emphasised that one saw them as partners in the evaluation, with full regard for their professional competence and doubts.

This is clearly an important principle for effective follow-up meetings, whether their function is to review the course and its results, to deepen understanding and reinforce the skills acquired or to extend acceptance of staff support as a human resource in the institution. All these uses confirm the teachers both as independent practitioners and as supportive members of an educational team – which may sometimes at least find it useful to invite somebody else as a reinforcer or a fresh stimulant. The outside consultant, however, will have to be careful not to become almost a member of the institution, so as not to lose the valuable outsider perspective. At its best, a school staff, with the help of their specialist colleagues, may soon take responsibility for their own in-service support training, and the staff may become capable of professional self-regulation and development, in tune with evolving demands and needs.

At this point we can summarise the role and tasks of a consultant to teachers and of the special needs, pastoral or curriculum coordinator in the school wishing to develop teacher support facilities with his colleagues.

Role and tasks of consultant facilitators

Whether he is a specially assigned professional development post-holder or pastoral colleague on the school's staff or contributes skills and experience from another institution and profession, his involvement as consultant can be variably active according to requirements and developments in the staff development group and will be influenced by his understanding of the group's preoccupations or 'basic assumptions' (Bion 1961). We have seen that in the initial stages the task is to establish a particular mode of working while acknowledging group members' expertise from the start and, in later periods of partial successes and disappointments, to continue to highlight latent strengths and to make the experience in the group usable professionally. Such periods call for greater participation, but in general the consultant meets the group members as partners and tries to participate equally with them. He must therefore forestall any semblance of wanting to tell others how to do their job and avoid the role of *sole* expert into which teachers may cast him in perpetuation of the perceived gap between them. His skill consists in not accepting this role – without thereby diminishing the value of the contribution that he is offering to make – and to forestall such ambivalent feelings as tend to arise when sole expertise is claimed by or attributed to one side in this field.

The consultant has to deal with these hazards from the beginning, by being prepared to learn from the teachers and to convey his understanding of the difficulties in their work setting and of how it can obstruct a teacher's ability to respond sensitively to children's emotional needs. This implies that one accepts the teachers' views of their difficulties as the essential and only possible starting point in a mutual pooling of expertise and that one does not ignore or override the knowledge which teachers have of child development and the learning process but perceives that knowledge as capable of supplementation. The consultant's special understanding can then be offered, not as superior, but as complementary and useful in the search for ways of helping children with difficulties to achieve sufficient sense of personal worth to participate more fruitfully in the educational enterprise.

We have seen how teachers can be helped to achieve this through an extension of their own skills, educational means and inner resources and how the consultant does not think it appropriate to offer clinical diagnoses or to teach a modified form of clinical-therapeutical treatment. He tries to enable them to see for themselves what difficulties there may be in a child's situation and how they might improve it by using educational means to help the child to cope better and to activate the therapeutic potential in curriculum content, delivery and relationships.

As we saw, the consultant's contributions are calculated to ensure that the explorations are focused on the child's actual behaviour and the responses it generated, on seeing it in the context of what was known about the child's circumstances and on gauging underlying needs and what provision of new learning experiences might help to meet them. These related to:

(a) the teacher's interaction with the particular child (such as acknowledging unintrusively what the child may be feeling or confronting him constructively with a difficulty, in a process of limit-setting and confidence building);

(b) consideration of the whole classroom group (to ensure new learning experiences with others);

(c) the therapeutic potential in the day-to-day curriculum as a source for such new learning experiences;

(d) the skills of involving other adults (parents or other professionals) as partners, in support of the teacher's objectives on behalf of the child.

As with similar support and training groups (see Gosling's (1965) analysis), to be able to make his contributions effectively the consultant to teachers needs firstly to be able to hear, non-judgementally and non-defensively, what they feel about their task and about himself. Secondly, he needs to create the exploratory climate in which these feelings can be used in support of the teachers' task. Thirdly, he needs to make his knowledge available in a way which is compatible with the overall purpose of the group, to enable the teachers to find their own most appropriate solutions to the cases examined as well as to all those others not brought up for discussion.

(i) The consultant as supportive recipient

The consultant's way of listening, of asking questions, of using his knowledge and of speculating about issues and consequences is designed to heighten awareness about people engaged in the educational process as teachers or pupils, whose personal background is likely to affect their participation in that process. This awareness is intended to facilitate the crossing of boundaries between them, without intrusion into a personal sphere which remains sacrosanct.

As active recipient of what is being communicated in the group, and by working from their perspective, the consultant allows himself to become 'educated' (as Steinberg (1989) puts it) about the members themselves, their work setting, their hopes, expectations and disappointments concerning their professional performance and especially about their painful emotions when they feel that they are failing with individual children.

At the same time, the consultant learns that he himself – like the group members in their role as teachers – experiences in sympathy powerful feelings of hope and disappointment. His method requires him to accept and work with these feelings in relation to the members' professional task rather than ignoring them or in other ways collusively re-enacting the teachers' own inappropriate behaviour. If the consultant succeeds in doing this, he may also be able to demonstrate authentic support – in response to professional rather than personal need – and so may help the teachers themselves to support children in special need, their parents or colleagues whose help they wish to enlist in aid of the child's educational progress.

The consultant is aware, however, that he is himself vulnerable to hazards which may make him less responsive and thus impair his ability to do this. Such hazards are, for instance, an excessive wish to be helpful, a fear of not being helpful enough and a wish to prove himself or to prove a point to a group. These may cause the consultant to make premature comments before he or the group can really understand the issue. He may give advice to teachers who perhaps already feel belittled by 'experts' and to whom he is supposed to show that, by having a fresh look at the situation, they may find some of the answers on their own.

Such advice may be seen as 'good' and, if applied effectively, may bring temporary, seemingly spectacular, results but may also lead to hazardous idealisation of the consultant. By 'helping' in this way the consultant will increase the teachers' doubts of their own sufficiency, whereas his aim is to reduce the grounds for these doubts and to build up their self-confidence. Moreover, admiration tinged with feelings of inferiority can, as we know, nourish envious ambivalence. Teachers may cherish for a time an idealised image of the consultant, which is likely to collapse at the first failure to achieve immediate results, giving place to disillusion and rejection of what he has to offer. Members may also lose faith in their own capacity to solve problems and fall back on the belief that there are no solutions – a belief which makes some teachers doubt and even appear to ridicule an offer of support to begin with.

The consultant will sometimes be tempted to side with either teacher or pupil against the other or to agree with both in seeing either the parents or the school as the cause of all the trouble. This, too, needs to be avoided, as it militates against non-judgemental exploration of the situation. It will be important for the consultant to make it clear that to acknowledge that negative feelings about children, or punitive actions, are understandable is not to approve of them and to insist that they must be examined as part of the situation. Failing this, his non-judgemental stance may be mistaken for approval. Another hazard is that, if he feels tired and drained in a session, he may fail to empathise sufficiently and may reel off his intellectual knowledge in unwitting collusion with those who use their intellectualism in defence against insight.

It is an essential part of this approach to recognise that such things happen in most teaching and learning relationships. The teachers will themselves, like the pupils, at one time or other have wished for more competence and yet resisted more knowledge for fear of its risks, will have dreaded incompetence and will have felt inadequate. However, they may have rejected this as part of both their own and their pupils' reality, instead of accepting such feelings as part, and part only, of all our selves and rediscovering those parts which want to learn and find new solutions. If the consultant can receive these feelings and give them recognition, with the authenticity of a professional prepared to use his own vulnerabilities and to be open about them in an unfussy task-related way, he may help the teachers in two ways. He may first help them to be able to own and accept their feelings and thus, secondly, to set energies free for competent performance as they discover that such recognition is a valuable means of getting through to children whose own anxieties have interfered with their progress at school. To the extent to which the teachers can themselves, like the consultant, become active recipients, they may become able to let children feel that they understand and accept their emotional uncertainties (as we saw with our teachers), make them bearable by such containment and help them to progress.

(ii) The consultant as creator of an exploratory climate

As we have seen, the consultative mode of working with support groups here described is introduced to the teachers as one of joint exploration within a relationship of coordinate interdependence. This way of working tends not to be a very prominent feature of hierarchical institutions, with their tendency to demand perfection from the leaders of institutions who in their turn tend to judge staff in accordance with similar demands. The consultant is likely to be the target of similar expectations – influenced, perhaps, by the 'high-' or 'low-' scale post that he holds on the staff – but any collusion with them on his part would either prolong the group's dependence or lead to a rejection of his actual abilities as falling short of the ideal. He must therefore emphasise from the beginning the cooperative nature of the venture, designed so that the teachers as autonomous professionals find for themselves, while supportive of each other, workable alternatives to solving the difficulties with which children's special needs confront them. We saw how the consultant has to aim at the first meeting to achieve general participation in a process of joint search. He has to create a climate of confidence which suggests to teachers that they can handle their own cases and that the only criteria for evaluation are derived from the task. To achieve an exploratory climate, the consultant should be careful not to act like the kind of teacher who is eager to offer answers when expected to do so, needs to listen to the questions which a presentation raises in the minds of the group members, must receive these questions with respect and must see to it that the differing expertise of each member, together with his own, becomes supportively available for the exploration.

He has to be alert to the likelihood of hidden agendas which militate against an exploratory climate in the form of misconceptions and erroneous expectations. This includes any ideas about offering 'therapy' which some members of the group may hope for or suspect. He does not define group or individual therapy as his task but has a duty to help both the children and the teachers in their professional role. To the extent to which the consultant succeeds in this, he may well, as Caplan first showed, help the group members indirectly, and often personally, and to that extent he may play a therapeutic role without setting out to do so. The experience of a genuinely exploratory climate may well be part of the 'therapy'.

(iii) The consultant as teacher and liaising assistant

Yet within this climate, the consultant has a teaching brief, which he may have to pursue quite directively.

Like other members of the group, he contributes his own complementary expertise: factual knowledge of child development and behaviour, and of disturbance-producing situations and the significance of various symptoms. He relates this to the educational context in which the teachers operate, extends their knowledge and skills and modifies their attitudes regarding the dynamics of families, classrooms and educational institutions as a whole and the interaction of teachers and learners. He adds his own professional way of looking at children to theirs, helping the teachers to define problems in interactional terms, and pools ideas of treatment alternatives which might help. The consultant can show how different approaches – within the teaching profession (teachers in secondary schools for instance are sometimes surprised by how relevant their infant and junior school colleagues' understanding is to the teaching of adolescents, and vice versa) and across professions – can be combined creatively in the teaching process when one thus focuses on underlying issues. He thereby helps them to stretch and define the limits of their role and responsibility more flexibly (a point which Maher (1985) for instance makes with regard to the school's response to juvenile crime), as he does with his own professional boundaries when redeploying his skills as consultant to groups of colleagues or interprofessionally.

As part of his boundary function the consultant helps the group to examine and develop the range of interactions within and across their professional boundaries – with members of the child's family and with professionals in the child care and other education services – and to discover how these may be better activated in the child's interest instead of interfering with it, as they sometimes do with unhappy consequences. As we saw in the case discussions, if the consultant's teaching brief includes focus on such hazards, and they are noted and understood in good time, they can be diminished or even forestalled. As has been shown, such teaching can take the form of both direct comments and indirect use of a group's here-and-now experiences, which may offer opportunities to develop better understanding and the skills needed to convert it into appropriate action. What the consultant does not do is to set out to change everything or tell people to do their job differently.

All schools are now required to have a staff development plan. Colleagues with cross-curricular special needs, pastoral, counselling or other special expertise could be enlisted, with the help of a liaising consultant, to promote some internal structure and procedure which may facilitate the development of an effective collaborative professional development system.

Such members of staff may themselves already be accepted by their colleagues as possessing such skills as might be useful to share. They would thus be able to act as consultants to pilot and extended groups (a training element in skills such as task-related activities with colleagues in their schools, for instance, forms part of the special needs courses of in-service training departments) which they succeed in initiating as just described and be helped by such guidelines as now exist to incorporate support work with colleagues. Alternatively, they may like to prepare the ground for such work in discussion with their colleagues and then, if enough of them agree, use their contacts with credible outside professionals to invite them to add their experience and expertise to that of the staff as temporary visiting consultants. As coordinators, they may convene a group of limited size but open to staff across the range of career experience, or one of key members of staff with whom it is hoped to build up the skills which they would need to run effective support groups with their colleagues. Consultants willing to do such work with teachers may be found in the network of external support services: child guidance units, school psychological services, special support and resource centres, special needs departments in higher education establishments. Special school staffs, too, can be invited to share with their mainstream colleagues their own expertise and depth of understanding.

Members of these services may lack experience in sharing their insights beyond their existing remit and may be diffident about assuming the role of consultant and may themselves need some support (see Chapter 9). They may be assisted to assume this role by the coordinator on the staff who can discuss with them how best to ensure a successful start to a developing support system in his school. This will involve cooperation with the outside expert as a professional colleague to help him to find the most acceptable and workable approach to adapt his expertise to the setting in which the teachers work so that they can make use of his understanding within the constraints of a classroom, thus extending their own skills and resources. The coordinator will have to impress on the consultant the importance of clarifying with the potential group at the outset what he would feel able to contribute as an outsider, what, together, they might reasonably expect to achieve and what ground rules would have to be agreed. The consultant will need to clarify with them the timing, frequency and minimum number of sessions needed to achieve these aims, who would be the core participants, what arrangements would be made for later or short-term attenders, what the pilot group itself might do to disseminate its experiences and what developments might be possible once the consultant's regular commitment expires. As we have seen throughout Part III, such considerations crucially precede actual work with the groups.

Through these advanced discussions with his colleagues and with the prospective consultant, the coordinator demonstrates his partnership skills, increases his credibility with colleagues and prepares the ground for effective teamwork. This makes it more likely that a staff development structure will become an integral feature in the continuing development of the staff's abilities to promote their pupils' learning capacities.

If coordinators in neighbouring schools can agree to recruit consultants in this way, the resources for supporting teachers will be greatly enriched. However, the potential consultants may themselves first wish to develop further their skills of support work with other professionals. Such experiential training in consultation skills is increasingly offered by in-service training departments in the form of short courses run on the case discussion model or as an integral part of modular award-bearing in-service courses, including those sponsored by voluntary professional organisations like the Forum for the Advancement of Educational Therapy and Therapeutic Teaching. Some school psychological services have also begun to develop a training role in consultation (Stow *et al.* 1992).

All such training in collaborative problem-solving, while focusing on the emotional and social needs of specific children, will enhance teachers' effectiveness as *teachers vis-à-vis* their other pupils. At the same time, sharing their experience and expertise as they explore their difficulties non-judgementally, without implying guilt or negligence, they experience how they, as genuinely enabling *colleagues*, can all contribute to each other's success.

As teachers, they deepen their understanding of children's difficult response as a reaction to difficulties as perceived; the extent to which such response is further influenced by the response it receives; and that this response is largely under the control of adults whose deepened understanding is now geared to enhancing their own ability to re-interpret, and to react to, a pupil's behaviour in such a way that a vicious circle of reinforced problem behaviour and resistance to learning can be broken (Upton and Cooper 1991).

As colleagues, they experience all the advantages of shared reflective practice, inquiry and collaboration which have been found to be the most distinguishing features of schools which aim to be effective for all their pupils (Ainscow 1991, Fullan 1982, 1992a, b).

How aware, however, are we of the training supporters' own professional needs to be able to ensure such effectiveness? This we shall consider in Chapter 9.

Chapter 9

Continuing Professional Development: Ongoing Support for Developing a Consultative Role

With a task of such importance and complexity, for both teachers and their staff development supporters, we must lastly address ourselves to the support and training needs of the supporters, and examine one more feature of a consultatively collaborative problem-solving model: its potential in providing much needed support for these supporters, if they are to operate effectively within and across schools and school services, to enable all staff to develop the 'skills, knowledge and understanding needed to make a reality of [the government's] proposals' of excellence for all children (DfEE 1997b).

Role shift and responsibilities: a mismatch between contrasting presumptions

Consultative collaboration has been outlined as a process of professionals exploring jointly a specific problem with the help of a non-directive facilitator in the consultative role. This role demands skills in the art of sharing one's own experience and expertise with fellow professionals as well as enabling them to share theirs with each other, to clarify the problem in such a way that they may find their own alternatives towards solving the problem.

In the context of this text the specific problem has been stated as increasing the competence of teachers *as teachers* to act on their recognition of emotional and social factors affecting children's learning capacity. Professionals specially qualified in the field of emotional, social and learning difficulties, who could assume the role of consultant, work in a range of external institutions, and of services and departments both within and across schools and school services. Traditionally, education and psychological services offered help to individual children away from the situation in which their difficulties occurred. Since the immediate post-Warnock decade, however, members of these services have been urged – and have begun – not to confine their attention to the few cases referred to them but also to address themselves to the problems of their teachers. The aim was to deepen the teachers' understanding of the interactive nature of emotional, social and learning needs, and to communicate this in such a way that it did not just reach the referred child but also those with whom he interacts in the classroom, as well as the many other children who would also benefit from this kind of understanding.

This meant a conspicuous shift in role and responsibilities. It required the experience of interprofessional skills to overcome the 'difficulty of historically contrasting presumptions' (Mongon and Hart 1989) which now confronted them: the contrast between their trained awareness that there are no ready-made answers, but that teachers have an unrealised capacity to deal more appropriately with many of the problems their pupils are facing; and the presumptions of teachers who are used to expecting from experts 'the answers to problems', and who therefore find the 'undramatic consultative, apparently understating approach to problems' so novel that they need some 'convincing before they can give it credibility' (Mongon and Hart 1989).

With their experience of both commonality and difference with regard to children's emotional and social needs these workers are aware that the learning and emotional difficulties experienced by some children may well point to more general problem areas in the classroom or school, and that learning to respond more appropriately and sensitively, both through curriculum content and delivery, to the more 'difficult-to-teach' pupils, can not only help to meet their needs but also enhance the quality of teaching and learning for the class, and ultimately for the school as a whole (Mongon and Hart 1989).

This perspective, whether held by those on the staff with a remit for staff development (DfE *Code of Practice* 1994, para. 2.26) or by institute staff development tutors or supporters from the external services, will not be shared by a number of colleagues with whom they are to work. Their work may involve them in assisting classroom teachers whose length of career experience may surpass their own (and has been known to be flaunted as such); who are specialists in subjects beyond the supporter's own expertise; who are ambivalent about 'having problems' and 'being seen as in need of help'; who are under pressure from many directions and feel they 'have no time to spare' to discuss individual children who 'shouldn't be in the school at all', for whom they demand some surface skills training to render them 'manageable', rather than teachers 'having to spend more time to help them' to manage their *learning*. Some teachers hope for a mere 'survival kit' as if this were sufficient to meet their professional needs (Hanko 1993b, 1994), but respond well to being introduced to strategies which strengthen their coping resources and the dynamic interaction between teacher and learners.

As we have also seen, school-based supporters may be faced with tensions between parents and teachers, and between members of staff within and across departments and management hierarchies. They may also meet with conflicting advice from different services. Any one of these factors may affect their effectiveness in the school. In addition, there are national contentions and pressures which may drive colleagues into conflicting stances detrimental to their professional task.

All of these are issues which need to be addressed by skilled supporters in the collaborative consultancy role. It requires well targeted *in situ* training provision that includes them as well as those with whom they are to work.

Joint problem-solving: attending simultaneously to the needs of pupils, teachers, the school and the supporters

We have seen how the consultatively collaborative problem-solving focus enables the group to attend simultaneously to the needs of both teachers and pupils. This multiple focus also singles it out as an effective way of supporting the supporters.

For the *school-based supporters* the approach is effective because its consultative design can release their skills to address both individual classroom and whole-school contexts – meet demands to pay immediate attention to the 'loudest' problems, but to do so in ways which generate insight into both problem solution and problem prevention, and thus mobilise a school's resources 'without necessarily disturbing, or being hampered by, [its] existing structures' (Mongon and Hart 1989). They proceed from supporting colleagues as individuals to helping them bring about whole-school policies on issues to be addressed by the staff as a whole.

Individual support consists of the staff group jointly exploring the opportunities that exist for them *as individuals* to attend to the affective dimension in children's learning through sensitive curricular adaptations, teaching approaches that take account of pupils perceptions of what happens to them in classrooms and how this affects their learning and behaviour, and the skilful enlisting of colleagues, specialists from other services, or parents – especially seemingly 'unhelpful' ones – as partners in facilitating a child's progress. Teachers also began in this way to develop skills of mutual support and negotiation through the group consultative approach. It is then only a step towards attending to those within-school factors which the *staff as a whole* needs to address.

The potential that lies in such a step by step progression is well demonstrated in Mongon and Hart's (1989) analysis of the initiatives which school-based supporters may be able to encourage. For it is they who are likely to need – at least initially – assistance of *staff from training institutions* or *the external services*. These supporting professionals in the consultative role, the supporters of the supporter, will themselves be sufficiently well versed in interprofessional consultative skills to be able to assist the school-based coordinators in the consultative aspects of their roles, and to facilitate a genuinely enabling process of joint enquiry, rather than merely offer their own solutions.

Such skills take time to develop, and it requires support to practise them in the face of the range of complexities that confront the specially assigned school-based coordinators. As Steinberg (1989) reminds trainer and would-be practitioners, it takes a little time to appreciate the essential *equality* in the consultative relationship. So much in the clinical, care, administrative and teaching fields is concerned with telling them what to do, albeit disguised in various ways, that the extent to which consultative work is a process of shared exploration of the matter in hand may not be apparent at first sight. To 'consult' is the word for what both consultant and consultee do, and both require skill to undertake it.

Reference has already been made to the apparently undramatic, understating, approach to problems and that its novelty requires to convince people of its efficacy before they can give it credibility. Such convincing – a consultative exercise in its own right – requires cumulative experience in consultation which newcomers to the practice cannot possess. Their problem is that they experience *concurrently* both their colleagues' disbelief in its value and their own tentativeness in practising it. To provide such cumulative experience, support of the supporters will have to be itself consultative. It will also have to address both levels of skill development, that of the new 'consultants' (the school-based coordinator(s) and of their 'consultees' (the group members). It will have to be as task-oriented and *in situ* as the support they aim to offer their fellow professionals.

To what extent can consultation groups for school-based coordinators address simultaneously both levels of development? How can they ensure that members of these groups

(a) experience, practise and develop consultative skills in the supporters' own group;
(b) are enabled to transfer the practice to their task in the schools?

If the essence of the consultative process is the collaborative exploration of a problem experienced by a consultee, then any problem experienced by consultees as would-be consultants – such as the problem of newness and first use in their work with teachers – will have to be jointly explored, by the school-based coordinators and whatever staff from the education institutes and psychological services are assisting them to develop their consultative skills.

From the detail presented earlier and elsewhere (Hanko 1986, 1987b, 1989a, b), we can summarise the *aims* of this process as sharpening teachers' recognition of children's individual needs; deepening their understanding of them; and augmenting their ability to meet them within the ordinary teaching day.

We can summarise the *process* as one of enabling teachers to find their own solutions to the problems of dealing with children's learning and adjustment difficulties; pursued, not by telling them what to do, but by engaging in a process of an initially quick on-the-spot explorative look at the situation from the other person's perspective, and then extend it *together with* the consultant's, both, as Steinberg (1989) puts it, educating each other about the issues faced by the presenter of the problem.

The *skills* involved in moving the exploration forward – whether deployed with individuals or groups of colleagues – we saw as consisting of

- asking answerable, insight-generating questions, widening insights about a pupil's difficulties and underlying needs, and how these might be met within sensitively adapted curricular and relationship experiences; asking such questions in a genuinely exploring, non-judgemental, and therefore supportive way;
- gauging from the answers the teachers' strengths, building on them, accepting and supplementing – rather than supplanting – the teachers' expertise with the consulting supporter's and that of others in the group;
- eliciting information in such a way that it can help to highlight the issues underlying the situation that is being explored.

Answerable, insight-generating, non-judgmental questions are open questions which lead to joint non-defensive exploration. They are formulated by beginning 'Do you think...?', '*Could* it be that...?', '*What* might happen if one tried...?', in contrast to closed questions like 'Why don't you try...?' or 'Don't you think...?' which invite yes/no responses given to an expert who is colluding with being given the *sole* expert role. This is contrary to the role of a consultant who avoids such collusion. Consultatively enabling questions are based on an awareness of how language works, how communication processes become, or do not become, effective. It is not a matter of 'questioning' others but of asking questions in such a way that sophisticated ideas are made more accessible by clarifying, rearranging and supplementing them in the sharing process.

They are part and parcel of developing a consultative role.

Developing the consultative role: coordinators' joint training groups

To experience the efficacy of these 'undramatic' skills, and to practise and develop them, school-based coordinators need to be able to bring the difficulties they face in their work to such support groups of their own, designed to enable them, in their turn, to find their own solutions.

Amongst the difficulties support staff may find daunting and bring for consultation, we have noted the initial fear of losing credibility when faced with new tasks but old conflicting expectations. Both school-based post-holders and educational psychologists may confess to feeling anxious at appearing unwilling to meet the demand for ready solutions; or worse, at seeming unable to do so. They will present this difficulty to their own support group when they doubt their ability to make the consultation model work.

They may themselves display their ambivalent feelings about this seemingly 'slow' approach, feelings similar to those they encounter in the schools. Mixtures of hope and disbelief, anxiety and disappointment with advice not taken up, or frustration with 'resistant' teachers may lead them to demand similarly clear-cut, reassuring, and ultimately counter-productive, answers.

They are thus confronting their own consultant with the same problem, which he, however, will be skilled to contain, and in the process of containment help them to handle. Not being offered a hoped-for answer, but being helped to explore the context in which they may, for instance, feel they are 'failing' with 'uncooperative' colleagues, they can then *experience* how their own consultant's authoritative admission of not knowing immediate answers differs from 'not knowing one's job'; how a matter-of-fact explanation (that, before workable solutions can be found, a problem requires exploration in context) can be shown to be a supportive rather than negative refusal of the 'sole expert' role; and how their consultant, instead of losing credibility, in this way establishes it, and is able to move the exploration forward into a joint effort of understanding the problem context. They can then proceed in the process of joint exploration, to practise genuinely explorative questioning skills, and transfer them for use in their work setting between training sessions.

Sporadic difficulties experienced in the process of transfer can then be brought back to subsequent training sessions, to be looked at within the joint problem-solving framework.

Training skills of the coordinators' supporter

Supporting the coordinators in the consultancy aspects of their role necessarily involves their consultant in a similar transfer of skills.

We saw how all our case discussions (Chapter 3) aimed to assist teachers in finding ways of sensitively adapting the children's learning experiences to their needs, by activating a deeper understanding of the child's need and of possible ways of affecting the context in which it was being displayed. This was achievable to the degree to which the *teacher's own professional needs* were also recognised and indirectly met at the same time.

A school-based coordinator will need to understand that effectiveness in his work with colleagues depends on the extent to which he can appreciate and unobtrusively attend to both processes simultaneously. He has to appreciate how a child's problem may have become the teacher's, or how a problem in the teacher's situation may be reflected in the problem he experiences with a pupil. Reducing the teacher's anxiety about the pupil's problem and helping him to understand it better and to think about possible solutions can indirectly also help to relieve the teacher's problem. We saw how in Dave's case (pp. 35–8), Mr E's colleagues had first to be assisted unobtrusively to appreciate their fellow-teacher's difficulty in accepting their help, before he could become more accepting of Dave; how Vic's teachers (pp. 32–5) were helped to understand how tensions between them unwittingly re-enacted those which he experienced at home; how the teachers' reactions and feelings towards Teresa (pp. 24–7) and John (pp. 41–4), and those of Dipak's teachers (pp. 45–8) towards each other and their superiors, seemed to mirror the pupils' feelings. Both the pupils' difficulties and, indirectly, the teachers' had to be attended to.

If this is the essential component of a support worker's interprofessional effectiveness – requiring redeployment of his child-related skills while sharing them with other professionals – this must also be the essential aspect of the support he receives himself. The support worker needs help to appreciate how a child's problem may have become that of the teacher whom he is expected to help, but the teacher's problem may also have become that of the support worker: a frustrating difficult-to-teach-pupil may, for instance, have rejected the well meant efforts of his teacher, who in his frustration may then reject the support worker's help as dismissively as the child treated the teacher, both now feeling similarly useless (as happened in Mr E's case discussion). The support worker's trainer (i.e. the supporter's supporter) must be able to address this aspect (by way of asking insight-generating questions) in the here-and-now immediacy of the supporter's support-cum-training experience. In this way the support worker is helped to contain the teacher's feelings (for instance of uselessness) instead of colluding with them by feeling similarly rejected.

It is the immediacy of understanding, in their support group, their own parallel experience, which enables the supporters, firstly, to appreciate that the teacher who fails in teaching a failing pupil, or in motivating disheartened or disaffected children, is likely to experience similar feelings of failure and disaffection (so realistically 'storied' in James Kelman's *A Disaffection* (Kelman 1989)); secondly, to understand that when such feelings become too painful to tolerate, they may then be 'put into' convenient others, such as the supporter, so as to make him experience what the teacher wants to get 'rid of', building defences against these feelings to make the failure 'disappear'; and thirdly, that containment, non-collusion, by a 'significant' other person can help to make the feelings tolerable, restore objectivity about them, and thus help to address them.

Supported in this way, a supporter may learn no longer to feel defeated by a 'difficult-to-help' teacher of 'difficult-to-teach' pupils, towards whom he might otherwise have become counter-productively judgemental and prescriptive; or with whom he might have fallen into other such traps like assuming an unwanted 'rescuer' role, and then being at a loss how to offer support acceptably without further confirming a colleague's 'failure' in the eyes of the Head and the rest of the staff; or colluding with the myriad obstacles which can hinder his work with the children's teachers.

It is in the immediacy of exploring a fellow coordinator's difficulty in their own support group that supporters can, for instance, be alerted to the ways in which they may be creating or reinforcing such obstacles. Non-enabling old habits of 'A telling B what to do' may surface disguised as pseudo-questions ('Why don't you try...?') and 'I-think-he-needs...' statements. Their effect can be examined the moment they are made, together with more genuinely explorative alternatives, which can then be adapted to the consultancy aspects of the coordinators' role in the schools. Being themselves asked answerable, insight-generating, supportive questions like 'How might this teacher feel if one offered him...?', 'What are the things you could be positive about with her...?' help the support teacher to remain in charge of finding solutions to his own problem with colleagues in the school, and, in tandem, assist him to help those colleagues to enhance, in their turn, their work with the children without taking it over. This then ensures that decisions for sensitive adaptations in the curricular offer and classroom relationships will not be the supporter's but remain with the teacher, his autonomy enhanced, and partnership with fellow professionals strengthened accordingly.

The task for the support teachers' own consultant supporter is thus parallel to theirs, *vis-à-vis* a fellow teacher. The support teacher or coordinator may want to deepen a teacher's understanding of a 'difficult-to-teach' pupil, but may need to deepen his own understanding of a 'difficult-to-help' teacher. Coming to see a teacher's seemingly entrenched dismissiveness of suggestions for alternative solutions to his problems with pupils as perhaps a 'useful' way of surviving in an unappreciative world which dismisses his efforts, a support worker will be less in danger of seeming to be similarly critical and of reinforcing the defence.

Any of the difficulties listed earlier as facing special needs, pastoral, or staff development post-holders can be thus addressed in their support group. Those supported early in their new role are then more likely to handle them effectively.

Joint problem-solving: contributing to school policies

Enabling a maximum number of teachers to respond more appropriately to children's individual needs and difficulties by examining and attending to their context – instead of merely looking in the child for causes – will have an effect on the school as a whole and come to influence its policies. In-service support for the supporters thus helps them not only to develop and consolidate their own skills and to gain credibility in exercising them effectively but also to widen perspectives as to their potential contribution to the policies on a whole range of related issues which schools are developing to implement the National Curriculum, none of which are without their interactive aspects. Effective policies on special needs, pastoral care, multicultural education, equal opportunities and classroom management all have to do with encouraging good practice for all pupils. Such recognition underpins the consultancy aspects of the professional development model; that of the interactive aspects of all children's learning and adjustment needs, which need to be addressed; awareness that the learning situation itself has to be examined for its possible contribution to difficulties; and that otherwise the institution charged with securing full curricular access to all its children may itself put obstacles in their way.

Thus the consultative collaboration model can not only take account of how best to assist the school-based supporters in their primary task of promoting understanding of the factors that affect children's learning capacity and enabling their teachers to attend to these factors, but can also address the obstacles in the school as a whole which can diminish their effectiveness. If addressed, this will not just be beneficial to individual children, but will enhance the effectiveness of the school as a whole.

As we saw, however, recommendations can be interpreted in line with traditional or merely unexamined preferences. Schools need to be alerted to warnings about the consequences of narrow over-emphasis in the face of directives which may threaten the overall aim of achieving excellence for all. Different interpretations of official directives and reports (see Chapter 5 with regard to the National Literacy Strategy) can lead to either narrow, educationally constraining policies or to genuinely educative ones. Much will depend on how the schools themselves are being helped to use their best endeavours to ensure the latter.

Who, then, in the light of such complexities, would be in a position to fulfil the function of supporters' supporter, and what 'encouragement' might they need to do so?

Staff development tutors and educational psychologists: shared concerns and complementary expertise

The Green Paper on excellence for all children and its subsequent Programme for Action (DfEE 1998) refer to comments on the developing role of educational psychologists and the wide range of their responsibilities in 'areas such as strategic management, working with schools, curriculum issues and family therapy' (DfEE 1997b) and shows concern that 'a large part of their time is tied up in the process of statutory assessment' as diverting key resources from early intervention and from providing help and support to pupils when it is most needed.

Educational psychologists share this concern with staff development tutors from within schools and the training institutions. Thus, co-consultancy arrangements have been successfully attempted. Many educational psychologists have begun to incorporate interprofessional consultancy in their work, to modify environmental stresses as pupils are being helped to cope with them. Accounts of these developments have been offered by training institutions and psychological services (Armstrong and Galloway 1992, Creese et al. 1998, Dowling and Osborne 1994, Frederickson 1988, Graham and Hughes 1995, Gray et al. 1994, Stow et al. 1992, Turner et al. 1996, Wagner 1995). They reinforce recognition of teachers, schools and the support services as an important part of the remit of both the training institutions and of educational psychologists, requiring their assistance to address those within-school factors that may be impeding children's learning capacity instead of enhancing it.

As clinical psychologists and systems consultants point out (Campbell et al. 1989, Dupont and Dowdney 1990), there are professionals other than educational psychologists with skills to act as consultants to schools on needs of children in a context of organisational structures and working relations (see Chapter 7). But educational psychologists have direct access to all levels of the hierarchy within and across schools and school services within which to use their interprofessional skills and understanding of human behaviour, to facilitate and influence the kind of support network through which to recognise both children's and teachers' needs; and to help these to be perceived as wants, and help to create conditions favourable to attending to them within the structure of the school.

In recognition of this position, educational psychologists are increasingly expected as a matter of course to contribute substantially to in-service training of teachers and to support schools in developing and implementing whole-school policies, while evidence collected (e.g. the Elton Committee's (DES 1989), Bennathan (1994)) emphasises the effects of policies that fail to provide such ongoing support and training. Failure to support their staff in responding appropriately to pupils' emotional, social and learning needs and in coping with their own feelings and anxieties about 'difficult-to-teach' children, is shown as not only increasing children's difficulties but as hindering the all-round effectiveness of teachers and school. Without a staff development support network, teachers easily remain unappreciative of each others' complementary expertise (in contrast to the assistance we saw them derive from sharing it in collaborative problem-solving workshops).

Unattended staff concerns, as is well known, tend to latch on to other 'convenient' staff splits within and across departmental and managerial hierarchies, such as frequently remain unresolved between staff from merged schools with contrasting policies; or, especially in secondary schools, may reinforce educationally dysfunctional distinctions, like those between pupils with and without 'special needs' and between those with special 'educational' needs and with behavioural and emotional ones; (who may be 'exempted' from 'normal' teaching).

Similar distinctions may be made between academic and 'support' staffs' – academic being concerned with the 'normal' curriculum for 'normal' pupils; and there may be a further subdivision of support staff, expecting SEN staff to deal with achieving 'educational results' without also attending to the interactional, emotional and social context of learning failure, seen as the province of pastoral care and psychological services.

These splits are major difficulties for school-based coordinators who are expected to assist in the development of sound whole-school staff development policies, and add to staff stresses at a time of numerous new legislative demands meant to enhance the quality of teaching and learning for all. If the institution is to meet its task of full curricular access for all its children, it will need the tutorial understanding of children's learning needs and of interprofessional skills, to help it address staff conflicts and tensions, as well as the needs of its pupils, so that it may become a 'good enough' institution for staff and pupils alike. We have seen from examples earlier how conditions may be created which are conducive to such developments, without obtrusive exposure of 'trouble spots' or staff having to suffer loss of face.

Having direct access to all levels of the hierarchy, educational psychologists sufficiently well versed in interprofessional consultative skills are thus ideally placed – together with staff development tutors from training institutions, or on their own – to provide specialist coordinators in schools and support services with the kind of in-service support they need, and to meet the conditions listed in the introduction as essential to making it effective: namely, to be of immediate and long-term use in the classroom and school setting; to be genuinely explorative and enabling, and thus not perceived as deprecating criticism from which to withdraw into entrenchment.

Psychologists developing their consultative role may themselves be apprehensive of addressing the teachers' professional needs, or the needs of the school as an institution, lest this be perceived as transgressing their traditional professional boundaries. They may then be tempted to return to confining their attention mainly to the needs of specific children and to remedying their learning failure. They will then miss crucial opportunities for unobtrusively developing teachers' skills in considering any other children's interactional needs with staff and fellow pupils; for making those sensitive curricular adaptations that might help to meet a specific child's needs as well as those of the whole learning group; and for contributing to such school policies as could address all those within-school factors which psychologists as much as staff development tutors from training departments recognise as marring some children's progress, thereby failing to contribute to the 'creation of positive curricular, organisational, and social learning contexts' (Jones and Sayer 1988) as are now envisaged as part of their remit in the Green Paper on excellence for all (DfEE 1997b, and its Programme of Action (1998)).

Clearly, this confronts many psychologists, as it does their colleagues in schools and support services, with a considerable mismatch between the complexity of their task and insufficient training for it. The courses offered by training departments and psychological services already referred to will be able to pay attention to the psychologists' own in-service needs as they evolve, to enhance or update their consultative skills. It can also be achieved through co-consultancy training arrangements.

Developing expertise as co-consulting facilitators

As we saw with our case discussions, much of the psychologist's child-related expertise is capable of redeployment for work with fellow professionals. It may, however, require supplementing. Criticism has been directed at those who relate to the children's teachers mainly as prescriptive experts, who lack understanding of classroom practicalities and of the many constraints under which teachers work. Other psychologists may need to deepen their understanding of classroom and institutional dynamics, of the ways in which groups work and the means by which they can be helped to assume control over adverse conditions, in favour of those conducive to supporting their professional task.

Since it is the essence of the consultative process that consultant and consultees join their equal but differing expertise, and do so by working with the perspective and experience of the consultee whose work problems are being explored, both consultant and consultees are, as Steinberg (1989) put it, becoming 'educated' in each other's experience. Psychologists who engage with teachers and support staff in a process of problem clarification and problem-solving are thus in the position of learning from their consultees what needs to be understood about their conditions and constraints. They may, however, need some practice-led training to learn to use their 'ignorance' – the consultant's 'courage of not yet knowing' the answer (Balint 1957) – as a bonus. Others, constrained by such apprehensions as tend to accompany the crossing of traditional professional boundaries without as yet established credibility, also welcome some initially assisted experience in applying their psychological understanding to the training of facilitators of staff development teams in their schools (Stow *et al.* 1992, Stringer *et al.* 1992).

As we have seen, the convening consultant to school-based collaborative staff groups *uses as well as trains* members of the group in exercising the skills of asking genuinely explorative answerable questions, and of supplementing the presenting teacher's expertise with the consultant's and that of others in the group. As groups develop, an experienced consultant will be able to enhance this training aspect of consultation, so that members of an ongoing group, acquiring those mutual support and training skills which a consultative approach develops, gradually become supportive consultants to each other. Such sessions can then continue for the consultants themselves in their own work setting, like the kind of internal staff development now felt to be crucial for schools.

As there are no a priori rules for the composition of such staff groups within and across schools and school services other than those agreed when setting one up – any additional training needs of interested psychologists can be catered for at this stage. The groups described in this book were all working with one consultant only. As described elsewhere, however (Hanko 1989a, b), a consultant may suggest to the head teacher of a school planning a staff development programme to address a specific issue like children's learning needs, that an invitation be extended to its psychologist and members of the support services to act as co-consultants, with a view to extending their consultative experience.

In this way, a sophisticated 'sitting by Nellie' situation develops, which caters for practice in consultancy skills without requiring the co-consultant(s) to feel responsible for a group's progress. It also permits evaluation after each session between consultant and co-consultant as to how the group and the consultative process had been moved forwards; how understanding of the staff's difficulties and reactions has influenced the kind of support offered so that they could respond to it; how conditions evolved for staff to realise across divides that a collaborative approach and mutual support were not only possible but essential. The co-consultancy training experience thus uses the Caplan model (see Chapter 2) with third level dimensions. Not only may one indirectly help a teacher with his problem when enabling him to help a pupil (when the child's problem has become the teacher's), but similarly one may help a support worker and co-consultant when the teacher's problem has become the supporter's, as we saw with Mr E's Dave (pp. 35–8) making his teacher feel useless, who then rubbished his supporting colleagues competence; or Dipak's teachers (pp. 45–8) who momentarily doubted the consultant's usefulness. Any co-consultants unwittingly colluding with this process can then be helped to contain it with their 'trainer's' assistance. We have now been able almost effortlessly to add a co-consultant 'trainee' dimension.

A co-consultant already in touch with the school as part of his patch will in this way be able to develop his professional development role by remaining in regular individual or group consultative contact long after the initiating consultant's commitment to the school has ended. He may then himself initiate such consultation with his other schools, use his consultative experience with members of the support services working in the schools of his patch, and, to continue with his own co-consultancy skills development, take part in occasional 'topping up' workshops run on the case discussion model.

Chapter 10

Promoting a Coordinated Staff Development Structure: A Summary

We have considered a collaborative model of continuing professional development aiming to promote the insight of teachers into emotional and social factors which are seen as profoundly affecting all children's learning.

In the light of seemingly contradictory interpretations emanating from the legacy of past legislation with its unintended and potentially damaging consequences we have reviewed the growing concern that teachers' opportunities to attend to the emotional and social factors in children's learning have been severely reduced in recent decades and been considered as lying outside an academic remit, while an excessively competitive teaching climate is feared to have led to academic failure for too many children.

We have taken account of the growing advocacy that professionals with special expertise in meeting children's special emotional and social needs should include in their remit systematic work with teachers, to share their complementary experience and skills for the benefit of more pupils than those who are individually referred to them. Growing interest in such enablement has been gaining further momentum with the current drive to achieve excellence for all children, and the greater recognition of factors which can impede learning capacity.

We have seen that efforts to offer teachers the kind of support which may deepen their understanding of such factors and assist them to adapt their teaching approach are as yet insufficient, and we have considered the obstacles which often interfere with the provision of such support. It has become clear that it is ineffective for individual professionals from within or outside the school to deal solely with one child after another and simply to advise teachers what to do. This alone cannot take into account what goes on in their classrooms and why teachers often react to children's difficulties in unhelpful ways. The principles and skills with which the specialists treat such children have to be used differently if at least some of them are to become available to mainstream classroom teachers. The perceived conflict between academic and affective objectives and approaches has to be reduced, and teachers need to be alerted to the 'therapeutic' potential of educational activities. We have looked at how these specialists may deploy their skills flexibly and acceptably, with due regard to the nature of the obstacles militating against their efforts and to the factors which make for success in realising that potential.

An approach has been described by which suitably qualified professionals can, step by step, reach a maximum number of teachers through individual and group discussions in which they can gain additional knowledge and skills by focusing on the context in which they are to be used. In this way they can learn to cope with the emotional, behavioural and learning difficulties of more pupils and help the children themselves to cope better. A feature of the method was to discuss a specific difficulty in a way which took account of the teachers' need for both immediate and long-term help by gaining new insights into the effects of emotional and social factors in children's learning. This helped to optimise the teachers resources to design the new learning experiences understood as strengthening the children's capacity for learning.

Workers from the relevant disciplines, professions and institutions will have their own ways of marrying their expertise with that of teachers in a process of continuing professional development. The principles and skills involved in doing so effectively, however, will not differ fundamentally and need to be based – like those described here – on an appreciation of the setting in which teachers have to work. This means that such supporters should not see themselves in an *exclusive* expert role. They should be prepared to learn from the teachers whose knowledge and expertise they do not come to supplant but to supplement and enhance. They should understand the institutional realities of the schools whose staffs they are supporting if they want to help them to improve these realities, and they should accept the teachers views of their difficulties as being of paramount importance and essential starting points in the collaborative endeavour of pooling their expertise as autonomous professionals. The aim is to mobilise the teachers' own skills, educational means and inner resources to recognise what is improvable in the learning environment, i.e. to recognise and put into effect the affective/social elements in educational methods, curricular content and educative relationships.

This method focuses on the teachers' and the school's educational concern with every child, alerting teachers to the influence of situational factors on children's response to the school's learning programme and to the opportunities which they have, as teachers, together with parents and colleagues, to maximise their own effectiveness. The method is based on the inherent potential which can be activated in staff development groups which consist of a core of teachers willing to commit themselves to regular attendance of varying lengths, but is also open to any colleague to attend on an ad hoc basis to discuss any child's learning as the need arises. It thus takes account of evolving needs and the pastoral caretaking dimensions of the teaching task.

As an in-service programme of *general* staff development it caters at the same time for the specific professional needs of the participant teachers. It can take account of each participant's need for information and release of the skills necessary to put insights and principles into practice. It does so at the point at which a difficulty is experienced and permits it to be examined in follow-up discussions of evolving needs, with fellow teachers and a facilitator capable of redirecting perceptions. All are working together in such a way that the possible contributory factors can be looked at – including those of the school setting – and knowledge, attitudes and skills conducive to finding solutions can be extended for application both to a specific case and to similar problems as they arise. At the same time it enables key individuals on either side of the boundary between schools, school services and welfare network through better cooperation to overcome the incidence of separate and conflicting interventions.

As an in-service provision of *training*, the method accords with the requirements stipulated for appropriate professional development: to maintain the autonomy of professionals in a field where this is equally crucial to those who teach and those expected to learn from them; to include reflection on and application of the enhanced skills as close to the job as possible, on the spot and within the school context, in the form of school-based management which is both person-oriented and task-oriented. With the help of specially qualified fellow participants, teachers inform themselves and each other, update their expertise, sharpen their awareness of organisational and attitudinal obstacles and may enhance their performance without the easily counter-productive pressures of any merit-linked assessment procedures. They become aware of educationally wasteful habits and dysfunctional effects of conflicts between educational values, apparent demands of the system and approaches to school improvement, as well as the defensive strategies they may themselves be using.

The school-based nature of the arrangements, if carefully prepared, gives them the essential institutional support. It minimises the difficulties experienced by those who take courses elsewhere (while these are of value), in communicating to their colleagues what they have learned and in trying to apply the new knowledge in the old situation. Instead, it brings the new knowledge into the old situation, where it is shared, discussed and examined by colleagues, with correspondingly greater impact. This can create a climate of commitment to ongoing implementation: its school-based nature facilitates post-course support for the skills and aptitudes developed, in the form of intermittent follow-through meetings. It uses the inter- and intra-professional staff community as an in-service resource, which facilitates purposeful cooperation and the mutual support needed for implementation, by allowing teachers to discover their importance to each other as colleagues and collaborators – a source that tends to be neglected in traditional away-courses for isolated individuals. It thus goes some way towards meeting the demands of those who acknowledge the need for continuing professional development and towards demonstrating to a school its own potential for institutional self-renewal as an in-service training institution. Teachers learn more effective ways of asking for support, of supporting colleagues and of sustaining their ability for more appropriate response to new demands. Teachers thus experience themselves as actually contributing to each other's and their own effectiveness, which is clearly a vital function of any collaborative professional development programme that aims at excellence for all children.

As a method of *task-focused analysis* it permits dissemination of available research findings and theory, and critical application of advances made in the education and welfare network. These are relevant to all teachers both on account of the wide range of children in their classrooms who experience difficulties in or out of school and the substantial common ground shared by all children whatever their difficulties. With this approach, such information can be geared to the teachers' current experience and professional needs.

An additional bonus must surely be the economical way in which a collaborative approach can maximise existing resources in schools. As regards the wide range of specially qualified staff within and outside the schools, it asks them to develop their expertise along the staff development stipulations of new governmental documentation (DfEE 1997a, 1997b, 1998), to equip themselves with and exercise the support skills required for involving fellow professionals in examining the issues confronting them in their task.

At a time when many new initiatives are to be put into immediate effect for long-term benefit, investment in a programme which is both *pedagogically and psychologically* responsive to children's learning needs seems of great importance. First-hand evidence suggests that through this continuing process of professional development, teachers, the only professionals in daily contact with all school-age children, can increase their competence to enrich all children's learning, in fellowship with each other, and can at the same time prepare them for what the future may demand.

Appendix to Chapter 5

 **Chelsea Children's Hospital School**

Helping Children to Understand and Cope with their Feelings

A selection of books compiled by the staff of the Chelsea Children's Hospital School.

ALIENATION

Not Now Bernard, David McKee, Andersen Press Ltd
Gorilla, Anthony Browne, Julia MacRae Books/Walker Books
Never Satisfied, Fulvia Testa, North South
Bill's New Frock, Anne Fine, Methuen
My Dad Doesn't Even Notice, Mike Dickinson, Andre Deutsch/Julia MacRae

ANGRY FEELINGS

Bad Mood Bear Big Day, John Richard, Beaver
I Don't Want To, Sally Grindley and Carol Thompson, Methuen
Where The Wild Things Are, Maurice Sendak, The Bodley Head Children's
   Books
The Witch in the Cherry Tree, Margaret Mahy, Penguin Books
Little Lord Want It All, Nick Ward, Blackie
The Bossing of Josie, Ronda and David Armitage, Oliver & B
Ginger the Whinger, Wendy Smith, Macmillan
The Very Worst Monster, Pat Hutchins, The Bodley Head Children's Books
Alex and Roy, Mary Dickinson, Andre Deutsch Ltd
All I Ever Ask, Bernard Ashley, Orchard Books
Bad Mood Bear and the Big Present, John Richardson, Beaver
The Night the Animal Fought, Jesus Zaton, Mantra
Mine, Osram Hiawyn, Frances Lincoln
The Angel and the Wild Animal, Michael Foreman, Andersen Press Ltd
Two Monsters, David Mckee, Andersen Press Ltd

BULLYING

Willy the Wimp, Anthony Browne, Julia MacRae Books
The Camera Obscura, Hugh Scott, Walker Books
Bully, Yvonne Coppard, Red Fox
Blubber, Judy Blume, Piper Books
Rosie and the Pavement Bears, Susie Jenkin-Pearce, Hutchinson Children's
   Books

DEATH AND BEREAVEMENT

Badger's Parting Gifts, Susan Varley, Oxford University Press
Nobody's Perfect, Jenny Hessel, Hutchinson
Goodbye Max, Holly Keller, Walker Books
Fred, Posy Simmonds, Jonathan Cape
Underdog, Marilyn Sachs, Oxford University Press
Some of the Pieces, Melissa Madenski, Little Brown & Co
To Hell With Dying, Alice Walker, Hodder & Stoughton
Grandma's Bill, Martin Waddell, Simon & Schuster
Grandpa, John Burningham, John Bingham

FAMILY RELATIONSHIPS

Are We Nearly There, Louie Baum, Bodley Head
Bet You Can't, Penny Dale, Walker Books
The Pain and the Great One, Judy Blume, Heinemann
My Sister, Molly Delaney, The Bodley Head
Aren't You Lucky, Catherine Anholt, The Bodley Head
Peter's Chair, Ezrajack Keats, The Bodley Head
Daniel's Dog, JoEllen Bogart, Scholastic
The Big Alfie and Annie Rose Story Book, Shirley Hughes, Red Fox
Don't Worry, Grandpa, Nick Ward, Red Fox
Not in Here, Dad!, Cheryl Dutton and Wendy Smith, Red Fox
Wish You Were Here, Martina Selway, Red Fox
Horrace, Holly Keller, Random House Children's Books
Changes, Anthony Browne, Julia MacRae
Along Came Tom, John Prater, The Bodley Head Children's Books
Along Came Eric, Gus Clarke, Andersen Press Ltd
My Dad Takes Care of Me, Patricia Quinlan, D.W. Friesen & Sons Ltd
A Gift For A Gift, Marie Henry, Heinemann
Start Copying Me, Alicia Garciadil, Hutchinson
Janine and The New Baby, Jolette Thomas, Andre Deutsch Ltd
It's Not The End of The World, Judy Blume, Pan Macmillan
I Want To Be An Angel, Jamila Gavin, Methuen Children's Boooks
Underdog, Marylin Sachs, Oxford University Press
The One in The Middle Is The Green Kangaroo, Judy Blume, William
   Heinemann Ltd

The Visitors Who Came To Stay, Annalena McAfee and Anthony Browne, Hamish Hamilton Ltd

Where Has Daddy Gone, Trudy Osman and Joanna Carey, Hamish Hamilton Ltd

FEARS

Bad Boris and the Big Ache, Susie Jenkin-Pearce, Hutchinson Children's Books

Lights Off, Lights On, Anelise Taylor, Andersen Press Ltd

Not A Worry In The World, Marcia Williams, Walker Books Ltd

Sam's Worries, Maryann MacDonald, ABC

First Flight, David McPhail, Blackie

After Dark, Louis Baum and Susan Varley, Andersen Press Ltd

Alfie Gets In First, Shirley Hughes, The Bodley Head Children's Books

In The Middle Of The Night, Kathy Henderson, Walker Books Ltd

Lost, David McPhail, Little Brown & Company

You're In The Juniors Now, Margaret Joy, Faber & Faber

Teddy Bears Take The Train, Susanna Gretz and Alison Sage, A&C Black Ltd

Marlanne Dreams, Catherine Storr, Billing & Sons Ltd

A Cool Kid Like Me, Hans Wilhem, Simon & Schuster

Be Brave Billy, Jan Omerod, Dent

Mr Underbed, Chris Riddle, Beaver Books

The Bears Will Get You, Jenny Nimmo, Methuen

There's Something Spooky In My Attic, Mercer Mayer, Dent

I'll Take You to Mrs Cole, Nigel Gray, Andersen Press Ltd

The Happy Rag, Tony Ros, Andersen Press Ltd

I Don't Want To, Sally Grindley, Methuen

The Berenstain Bears In The Dark, Stan Berenstain, Random House

Franklin In The Dark, Paulette Bourgeois, Macmillan

Scary Story Night, Rob Lewis, Simon & Schuster

FRIENDSHIP AND TRUST

Best Friends, Steve Kellog, Hutchinson

I Hate Roland Roberts, Martina Selway, Red Fox

Alex and Roy, Mary Dickinson, Andre Deutsch

Just Like Us, Hiawaya Osram, Andersen Press Ltd

I Won't Go There Again, Susan Hill, Walker Books Ltd

Best Friends Worst Luck, Mary Hooper, Walker Books Ltd

In The Attic, Hiawya Oram and Satoshi Kitamvra, Andersen Press Ltd

On The Way Home, Jill Murphy, Macmillan Children's Books

Willy and Hugh, Anthony Browne, Julia MacRae Books

Rosie and the Yellow Ribbon, Paula De Paolo, Little Brown & Company (Canada)

GREED

Wish What, Alex Brychta, Oxford University Press

IMAGINATION

In The Attic, Hiawyn Oram, Andersen Press
On The Way Home, Jill Murphy, Macmillan
The Tiger Who Came To Tea, Judith Kerr, Collins

IMAGINARY FRIENDS AND COMFORTS

Oscar Got The Blame, Tony Ross, Andersen Press
Aldo, John Burningham, Jonathan Cape Ltd
Alfie Gives a Hand, Shirley Hughes, The Bodley Head Children's Books
Dogger, Shirley Hughes, The Bodley Head Children's Books
Anyone Seen Harry Lately?, Hiawyn Oram and Tony Ross, Andersen Press
Having Friends, Leila Berg, Methuen
There's A Hippopotamus On The Roof Eating Cake, Hazel Edwards, Knight
Geraldine's Blanket, Holly Keller, Hippo
Crocodarling, Mary Rayner, Lions

INDIVIDUALITY – BEING YOURSELF

Would You Rather, John Burningham, Jonathan Cape Ltd
Ruby, Maggie Glen, Hutchinson
Michael, Tony Bradman and Tony Ross, Andersen Children's Books
Amazing Grace, Mary Holfman and Caroline Binch, Frances Lincoln Ltd
Nancy Know Size, Mary Holfman and Jennifer Northway, Methuen Children's
    Books/Mammoth
Tidy Titch, Pat Hutchins, Julia MacRae Books
You'll Soon Grow Into Them, Titch, Pat Hutchins, The Bodley Head Children's
    Books
Daley B, Jon Blake and Axel Scheffier, Walker Books Ltd
Elmer, David McKee, Red Fox
I Want To Be An Angel, Jamila Gavin, Methuen Children's Books
Otto is Different, Franz Bradenburg, Julia MacRae
Would You Rather, John Burningham, Lions
The Paper Bag Princess, Robert N. Munsch, Hippo
William's Doll, Charlotte Zolotow, Harper and Row

LONELY FEELINGS

Gorilla, Anthony Browne, Julia MacRae Books
Willy & Hugh, Anthony Browne, Julia MacRae Books
Louie, Ezrajack Keats, Hamish Hamilton

Making Friends, Margaret Nahy, Puffin
Them And Us, Jennifer Curry, Red Fox

DISABILITY

The Bus Stop People, Rachel Anderson, Oxford University Press

REFUGEES EXPERIENCE OF WAR

The Peacock Garden, Anita Desai, William Heinemann

STRANGER DANGER

Your Guess Is As Good As Mine, Bernard Ashley, Julia MacRae Books

TRUANCY

King of Spuds, Jean Ure, Orchard Books

Bibliography

Abercrombie, M. I. J. (1969) *The Anatomy of Judgment*. London: Hutchinson

Aggarval, P. and McGonagle, B. (1996) *Community links with Primary Schools*. London: Chelsea Children's Hospital School.

Ainscow, M. (1991) *Effective Schools for All*. London: David Fulton Publishers.

Alvarez, A. and Phillips, A. (1998) 'The importance of play', *Child Psychology and Psychiatry Review* 3(3), 99–103.

Archer, M. (1998) 'Affirmative action', *Special Children* 111, 27–9.

Armstrong, D. and Galloway, D. (1992) 'Who is the child psychologist's client?', in ACPP *Newsletter* 14(2). Association of Child Psychology and Psychiatry.

Baker, K. and Sikora, J. (1982) *The Schools and In-service Teacher Education (SITE) Evaluation Project*. University of Bristol School of Education.

Balint, M. (1957) *The Doctor, His Patient and the Illness*. London: Pitman Medical.

Ball, M. (1998) 'Relationships between school, family and the community', *Findings*, June. York: Joseph Rowntree Foundation.

Barkley, R. A. (1997) *Defiant Children: A Clinician's Manual for Assessment and Parent Training*. New York: Guilford Press.

Barnes, D. (1976) *From Communication to Curriculum*. Harmondsworth: Penguin.

Barnett, B. and Parker, G. (1998) 'The Parentified Child: Early Competence or Childhood Deprivation?' *Child Psychology & Psychiatry Review* 3(4), 146–55.

Barrett, M. and Trevitt, J. (l991) *Attachment Behaviour and the Schoolchild*. London: Routledge.

BBC Radio 3 (1998) 'The Politics of the Romantic Hero', 12 August.

Bennathan, M. (1994) 'What more can we do?' *Special Children* 71, 19–22.

Bennett, N. (1991) 'Co-operative learning in classroom processes and outcomes', *Journal of Child Psychology and Psychiatry* 32(4), 581–94.

Berger, M. (1979) 'Behaviour modification in education and professional practice: the dangers of a mindless technology', *Bulletin of the British Psychological Society* 32.

Bettelheim, B. (1985) *The Uses of Enchantment*. Harmondsworth: Penguin.

Bion, W. (1961) *Experiences in Groups*. London: Tavistock.

Bion, W. (1962) *Learning from Experience*. London: Heinemann.

Bion, W. (1970) *Attention and Interpretation*. London: Tavistock.

Black, D. (1983) Impact of Bereavement on Children. ACPP Paper delivered at the Institute of Child Health, London, June.

Black, P., Brown, M., Simon, S. and Blondel, E. (1996) 'Progression in learning: issues and evidence in mathematics and science', in Hughes, M. (ed.) *Teaching and Learning in Changing Times*. Oxford: Blackwell.

Blair, T., PM (1998) 'Forging an inclusive society', *Times Educational Supplement*, 11 September, 26.

Boseley, S. (1997) 'The despair of bullied schoolboys', *Guardian*, 28 February, 5.

Bowlby, J. (1979) 'On knowing what you are not supposed to know and feeling what you are not supposed to feel', *Forum for the Advancement of Educational Therapy, Supplement 14*.

Bowlby, J. (1985) 'Foreword', in Dowling, E. and Osborne, E. (eds) *The Family and the School*. London: Routledge and Kegan Paul.

Bowlby, J. (1988) *A secure base. Clinical applications of attachment theory*. London: Routledge.

Boyle, J. (1977) *A Sense of Freedom*. Edinburgh: Canongate.

Breakwell, G. M., Collie, A., Harrison, B. and Propper, C. (1984) 'Attitudes towards the unemployed: effects of threatened identity', *British Journal of Social Psychology* 23(2).

Britton, R. (1981) 'Re-enactment as an unwitting professional response to family dynamics', in Box, S. (ed.) *Psychotherapy with Families*. London: Routledge and Kegan Paul.

Brock, P. (1984) 'Unemployment much more than an economic and social ill', *Guardian*, 25 April.

Bruner, J. S. (1961) 'The Act of Discovery', *Harvard Educational Review* 31(1).

Bruner, J. S. (1968) *Toward a Theory of Instruction*. New York: Norton.

Burns, R. (1982) *Self-concept Development and Education*. London: Holt, Rinehart and Winston.

Campbell, D., Draper, R., Huffington, C. (1989) *A Systematic Approach to Consultation*. London: DC Associates.

Caplan, G. (1961) *An Approach to Community Mental Health*. London: Tavistock.

Caplan, G. (1970) *The Theory and Practice of Mental Health Consultation*. New York: Basic Books.

Caplan, G. (1982) 'Introduction' to Schulberg, H. C. and Killilea, M. (eds) *Modern Practice of Community Mental Health*. New York: Jossey Bass.

Caspari, I. (1974) 'Parents as co-therapists'. International Congress of Child Psychiatry, Philadelphia.

Caspari, I. (1975) 'A psychodynamic view of the therapeutic opportunities of special education', in Wedell, K. (ed.) *Orientations in Special Education*. Chichester: Wiley.

Children's Express (1998) *By Children for Everyone*. London: London Bureau. Exmouth House.

Clarke, C. (1998) 'Assessment of infants not linked to setting', *Times Educational Supplement*, 11 September, 26.

Clark, C., Dyson, A., Millward, A. J. and Skidmore, D. (1997) *New Directions in Special Needs: Innovations in Mainstream Schools*. London: Cassell.

Claxton, G. (1998) *Hare Brain: Tortoise Mind: Why Intelligence Increases When You Think Less*. London: Fourth Estate.

Clements, A. (1998) 'How Prokofiev was cornered into a celebration of "glorious" revolution', *Guardian*, 11 August.

Collins, J. (1996) *The Quiet Child*. London: Cassell.

Collins, J. (1998a), *Playing truant in mind: the social exclusion of quiet pupils*. Milton Keynes: Open University School of Education.

Collins, J. (1998b), Enabling Teachers to 'Hear' Pupils' and Parents' Unheard Voices. Paper delivered at a Conference of the Forum for the Advancement of Educational Therapy and Therapeutic Teaching, London, 16 May (unpublished).

Cooper, P., Smith, C. J. and Upton, G. (1994) *Emotional and Behavioural Difficulties*. London: Routledge.

Creese, A., Norwich, B., Daniels, H. (1998) 'The prevalence and usefulness of collaborative teacher groups', *Support for Learning* 13(3), 109–14.

Crompton, M. (1980) *Respecting Children*. London: Arnold.

Daines, R. (1981) *Child Guidance and Schools: A Study of a Consultation Service*. Department of Social Work, School of Applied Social Studies, University of Bristol.

Dakers, S. (1998) 'Board stupid'. *Guardian*, 2 September, 9.

Daniels, H. (1993) 'The individual and the organization', in Daniels, H. *Charting the Agenda*. London: Routledge.

Daniels, H. (1996) 'Back to basics', *British Journal of Special Education* 23(4), 155–61.

Davie, R. and Galloway, D. (eds) (1996) *Listening to Children in Education*. London: David Fulton Publishers.

Davie, R., Upton, G., Varma V. (eds) (1996) *The Voice of the Child*. London: Falmer Press.

Davies, G. (1983) *Practical Primary Drama*. London: Heinemann.

Department for Education (DfE) (1994) The Education of Children with Emotional and Behaviour Difficulties (Circular 9). London: HMSO.

Department for Education and Employment (DfEE) (1997a) *Excellence in Schools*. London: HMSO.

Department for Education and Employment (DfEE) (1997b) *Excellence for All Children*. London: Stationery Office.

Department for Education and Employment (DfEE) (1997c) *Draft Guidance on LEA Behaviour Support Plans*. DfEE Publications.

Department for Education and Employment (DfEE) (1998a) *The National Literacy Strategy – A Framework for Teaching*. DfEE Publications.

Department for Education and Employment (DfEE) (1998b) *The New Start Strategy: Engaging the Community*, West, A. and Ciotti, M. (eds). London: Community Development Foundation Publications.

Department for Education and Employment (DfEE) (1998c) *Meeting Special Educational Needs – A Programme of Action*. DfEE Publications.

Department of Education (DfE) (1994) *Code of Practice on the Identification and Assessment of Special Educational Needs*. London: HMSO.

Department of Education and Science (DES) (1989) *Discipline in Schools* (Elton Report). London: HMSO.

Department of Health (DoH) (1998) *Working Together to Safeguard Children*. Wetherby: Social Care Group Department of Health.

Devlin, A. (1997) *Criminal Classes. Offenders at School*.   Winchester: Waterside Press.

Dixon, A. (1998) 'Whatever happened to the lively lads?', *Times Educational Supplement*, 27 March, 14.

Dockar-Drysdale, B. (1973) *Consultation in Child Care*. London: Longman.

Dowling, E. (1994) 'Theoretical framework: a joint systems approach to educational problems with children', in Dowling, E. and Osborne, E. (eds) *The Family and the School*. London: Routledge.

Dowling, E. and Osborne, E. (1994) *The Family and the School: A Joint Systems Approach to Problems with Children*, 2nd edn. London: Routledge.

Dupont, S. and Dowdney, L. (1990) 'Dilemmas in working with schools', Association for Child Psychology and Psychiatry *Newsletter* **12**(1).

Eggleston, J. (1977) *The Ecology of the School*. London: Methuen.

Elliott, J. (1982) 'The idea of a pastoral curriculum', *Cambridge Journal of Education* **12**(1).

Erikson, E. H. (1964) *Childhood and Society*. Harmondsworth: Hogarth with Pelican.

Erikson, E. H. (1980) *Identity and the Life Cycle*. New York: Norton.

Evans, J. (1990) Developing multi-professional and inter-agency co-operation. Paper delivered at International Special Education Congress, Cardiff.

Evans, P. (1993) 'Some implications of Vygotsky's work for special education', in Daniels, H. *Charting the Agenda*. London: Routledge.

Eyre, D. (1997) *Able Children in Ordinary Schools*. London: David Fulton Publishers.

Fagot, B. I. and Leve, L. D. (1988) 'Teacher ratings of externalising behaviour at school entry', *Journal of Child Psychology and Psychiatry* **39**(4), 555–66.

Ferri, E. (1984) *Stepchildren*. Windsor: NFER Nelson.

Fitzherbert, K. (1977) *Childcare Services and the Teacher*. London: Temple Smith.

Flood, S. (1998) 'Dismantling the Berlin Wall', *Young Minds Magazine* **35**, 7.

Frederickson, N. (1988) 'Continuing professional education: towards a framework for development', in Jones, N. and Sayer, J. (eds) *Management and the Psychology of Schooling*. London: Falmer Press.

Freeman, J.(1996) 'Talent will out', *Times Educational Supplement*, 30 August.

Fullan, M. (1982) *The Meaning of Educational Change*. New York: Teachers College Press.

Fullan, M. (1992a, b) 'School improvement: the challenge of change', *Times Educational Supplement*, 9 October, and London Institute of Education Lecture, 12 October.

Ghouri, N. (1998) 'Mums too afraid to ask', *Times Educational Supplement*, 4 September.

Gold, K. (1998) 'Taking it as red', *Times Educational Supplement*, 6 March.

Goldacre, P. (1980) 'Helping children with bereavement', *Therapeutic Education*, **8**(2).

Gorman, T. (1998) 'Every minute counts', *Times Educational Supplement*, 22 May.

Gosling, R. (1965) *The Use of Small Groups in Training*. London: Codicote Press.

Graham, P. and Hughes, C. (1995) *So Young, So Sad, So Listen*. London: Gaskell/West London Health Promotion Agency.

Gray, P. and Dessent, T. (1993) 'Getting our Act Together', in *British Journal of Special Education* **20**(1).

Gray, P., Miller, A., Noakes, J. (1994) *Challenging Behaviour in Schools*. London: Routledge.

Green, M. (1996) 'Using fairy tales with children', *Educational Therapy and Therapeutic Teaching* **5**, 18–35.

Greenhalgh, P. (1994) *Emotional Growth and Learning*. London: Routledge.

Griffiths, C. (1998) 'Literacy and the SENCO', *Special Children* **109**, Supplement, 1–5.

Grove. N. and Park, K. (1996) *Odyssey Now*. London: Jessica Kingsley Publishers.

Hanko, G. (1985) *Special Needs in Ordinary Classrooms. An Approach to Teacher Support and Pupil Care*. Oxford: Blackwell.

Hanko, G. (1986) 'Social workers as teacher consultants', *Journal of social work practice* **2**(2).

Hanko, G. (1987a) 'Group consultation with mainstream teachers', in Thacker, J. (ed.) *Working with Groups*, 123–30. *Educational and Child Psychology* **4**(3,4). Leicester: British Psychological Society.

Hanko, G. (1989a) 'After Elton: how to 'manage' disruption?', *British Journal of Special Education* **16**(4) 140–43.

Hanko, G. (1989b) 'Sharing expertise: developing the consultative role', in Evans, R. (ed.) *Special Educational Needs: Policy and Practice*. Oxford: Blackwell.

Hanko, G. (1991) 'Breaking down professional barriers' (The 1990 David Wills Lecture), *Maladjustment and Therapeutic Education* **9**(1), 3–15.

Hanko, G. (1993a) 'Staff Development and Support', *Support for Learning* **8**(4), 174–7.

Hanko, G. (1993b) '"The Right to Teach": but what are Lee Canter's children learning?', *British Journal of Special Education* **20**(29), 71.

Hanko, G. (1994) 'Discouraged Children: when praise does not help', *British Journal of Special Education* **21**(4), 166–8.

Hanko, G. (1995) *Special Needs in Ordinary Classrooms: From Staff Support to Staff Development*, 3rd edn. London: David Fulton Publishers.

Hargreaves, D. H. (1972) *Interpersonal Relations and Education*. London: Routledge and Kegan Paul.

Hart, S. (1996) *Beyond Special Needs*. London: Paul Chapman Publishing.

Heaney, S. and Hughes, T. (1997) *The School Bag*. London: Faber and Faber.

Hider, A. T. (1981) *The SITE Project in Ealing 1978–1980*. University of Bristol School of Education Research Unit.

Hillman, J. (1998) 'The myths of disaffection. Wasted Youth Report', *Times Educational Supplement*, 17 July, 13.

Holditch, L. (1985) 'Bridge building between teachers and social workers', in Dowling, E. and Osborne, E. (eds) *The Family and the School*, 177–187. London: Routledge and Kegan Paul.

Holland, V. (1998) 'Understanding boys: problems and solutions', *Support for Learning* **13**(4), 174–78.

Hoyles, C. and Neumark, V. (1998) 'Nursing by numbers', *Times Educational Supplement*, 13 March, 22–5.

Hughes, T. (1998) *Birthday Letters*. London: Faber and Faber.

Irvine, E. E. (1959) 'The use of small group discussions in the teaching of human relations and mental health', *British Journal of Psychiatric Social Work* **6**.

Irvine, E. E. (1979) *Social Work and Human Problems*. Oxford: Pergamon.

Jackson, S. (1987) *The Education of Children in Care*. University of Bristol School of Applied Social Sciences.

Jackson, S. (1988) 'The escape hatch that stays locked', *Times Educational Supplement*, 27 May, 10.

Jackson, S. (1994) 'Educating children in residential and foster care', *Oxford Review of Education* **20**(3), 267–79.

James, C. (1980) *Unreliable Memoirs*. London: Picador.

Jones, N. and Sayer, J. (1988) *Management and the Psychology of Schooling*. London: Falmer Press.

Kahn, J. and Wright, S. E. (1980) *Human Growth and the Development of Personality*, 3rd edn. Oxford: Pergamon.

Kelman, J. (1989) *A Disaffection*. London: Secker and Warburg.

Kolvin, I., Garside, R. E., Nicol, A. R., Macmillan, A., Wolstenholme, E. and Leitch, I. M. *Help Starts Here*. London: Tavistock.

Lacey, P. and Lomas, J. (1993) *Support Services and the Curriculum*. London: David Fulton Publishers.

Lanyado, M. (1989) 'United We Stand...?', *Maladjustment and Therapeutic Education* **7**(3), 136–46.

Laslett, R. and Smith, C. (1984) *Effective Classroom Management*. London: Croom Helm.

Leicestershire Library and Information Service (no date given) *Help at Hand, a selection of books to help young children deal with special situations*.

Levine, J. (1993) 'Learning English as an additional language in multilingual classrooms', in Daniels, H. *Charting the Agenda*. London: Routledge.

Lewis, M. M. (1963) *Language, Thought and Personality in Infancy and Childhood*. London: Harrap.

Lindsey, C. (1985) 'Some aspects of consultation to primary schools', in Dowling, E. and Osborne, E. (eds) *The Family and the School*. London: Routledge and Kegan Paul.

Macgonagle, N. (1993) *Lifelines*. Harmondsworth: Penguin.

Madge, M. N. (1983) 'Unemployment and its effects on children', *Journal of Child Psychology and Psychiatry* **24**(2).

Maher, P. (1985) 'The frontiers of teacher responsibility', *Pastoral Care in Education* **3**(1).

Maines, B. and Robinson, G. (1991) 'Don't beat the bullies!', *Educational Psychology in Practice* **7**(3), 168–172.

Maines, B. and Robinson, G. (1992) *The No Blame Approach to Bullying*. Bristol: Lucky Duck.

Marland, M. and Rogers, R. (1997) *The Art of the Tutor*. London: David Fulton Publishers.

McGill, P. (1998) 'Homework with added spice', *Guardian Education*, September, 9.

Milgram, S. (1974) *Obedience to Authority*. London: Tavistock.

Mittler, P. and Mittler, H. (1982) *Partnership with Parents*. National Council for Special Education, Developing Horizons Series 2.

Mongon, D. and Hart, S. (1989) *Improving Classroom Behaviour*. London: Cassell.

Morris, B. (1965) 'How does a group learn to work together?', in Niblett, W. R. (ed.) *How and Why do we learn?* London: Faber and Faber.

Morris, B. (1991) 'The Nature and Role of Educational Therapy', *Journal of Educational Therapy* **3**(3), 5–14.

Mosley, J. (1993) *Turn Your School Round*. Wisbech, Cambridgeshire: Learning Development Aids (LDA).

National Association for the Care and Rehabilitation of Offenders (NACRO) (1998) *Directing People from Crime: A guide based on the Northamptonshire experience of working in partnership*. London: NACRO Publications.

National Curriculum Council (1989) *Curriculum Guidance 2. A Curriculum for All*. York: NCC.

National Literacy Association (1998) *Out of The Bag*. Birmingham: Questions Publishing.

Newton, T. and Wilson, D. (1996) 'Circles of Friends', *Educational Psychology in Practice* **12**(1).

NHS Health Advisory Service (1995) Child and Adolescent Mental Health Services Thematic Review: 'Together we stand', paras. 246/9, 274/7. London: HMSO.

Norwich, B. (1996a) Special needs education or education for all. Connective specialisation and ideological impurity, *British Journal of Special Education* **23**(3), 100–103.

Norwich, B. (1996b) 'Special needs education, inclusive education or just education for all?' Inaugural Lecture, Institute of Education University of London.

Norwich, B. (1998) *Future Policy for SEN: Responding to the Green Paper*. NASEN.

Nunes, T. (1998) *Developing children's minds through literacy and numeracy*. University of London Institute of Education.

Oakeshott, E. (1973) *The Child under Stress*. London: Priory.

O'Brien, T. (1998a) 'Putting the Child First', *Special Children*, April, 12–15.

O'Brien, T. (1998b) *Promoting Positive Behaviour*. London: David Fultin Publishers.

Osborne, E. (1994) 'The teacher's view. Working with teachers out of the school setting', in Dowling, E. and Osborne, E. *The Family and the School*, 102–11, 2nd edn. London: Routledge.

Osborne, E. (1998) 'Learning cultures', in Davou, B. and Xenakis, F. (eds) *Feeling, Communicating and Thinking*, 35–53. Athens: Papazissis Publishers.

Pagani, L., Tremblay, R. E. *et al.* (1998) 'The impact of family transitition on the development of delinquency', *Journal of Child Psychology and Psychiatry* **39**(4), 489–99.

Palmer, S. (1998) 'Rainy Days. Project literacy hour', *Times Educational Supplement*, 23 March, 27.

Pelleschi, A. (1985) 'Pastoral care and girls of Asian parentage', *Pastoral Care in Education*, **3**(2).

Peter, M. (1995) *Making Drama Special*. London: David Fulton Publishers.

Peters, R. S. (1974) 'The education of the emotions', in Peters, R. S. (ed.) *Psychology and Ethical Development*. London: Allen and Unwin.

Phillips, A. (1998) 'It's just so unfair', *TES Magazine* **13**(11), 14–15.

Pollard, A. (1993) 'Learning in primary schools', in Daniels, H. *Charting the Agenda*. London: Routledge.

Pugh, G., DeAth, E., Smith, C. (1994) *Confident Parents, Confident Children*. London: National Children's Bureau.

Puura, K., Almquist, F. *et al.* (1998) 'Children with symptoms of depression: what do adults see?' *Journal of Child Psychology and Psychiatry* **39**(4), 577–585.

Quinton, D. (1987) 'The consequences of care', *Maladjustment and Therapeutic Education* **5**(2).

Quinton, D. and Rutter, M. (1983) 'Parenting behaviour of mothers raised in care', in Nicol, A. R. (ed.) *Practical Lessons for Longitudinal Studies*. Chichester: Wiley.

Quinton, D. and Rutter, M. (1987) *Parenting Breakdown*. Avebury.

Quinton, D., Rushton, R., Treseder, J. (1990) New parents for older children. Paper delivered at Association for Child Psychology and Psychiatry Conference.

Redl, F. (1966) *When We Deal with Children*. New York: Free Press.

Redl, F. and Winemann, D. (1957) I. *Children Who Hate*. II. *Controls from Within*. New York: Free Press.

Redwood, F. (1998) 'The sins of the fathers' (Save the Children Report, *Working with Children of Prisoners*), *Special Children* **113**, 9–10.

Reik, T. (1947) *Listening with the Third Ear*. London: Allen and Unwin.

Rice, A. K.(1971) *Learning for Leadership: Interpersonal and Intergroup Relations*. London: Tavistock.

Roaf, C. and Lloyd, C. (1995) 'The welfare network: how well does the net work?', Oxford Brookes University and Joseph Rowntree Foundation, *Findings*.

Roberts, J. (1995) *Dear Psychiatrist...Do Child Care Specialists Understand?* Cambridge: Lutterworth Press.

Rutter, M. (1975) 'Family and school influences on behavioural development', *Journal of Child Psychology and Psychiatry* **27**(3).

Rutter, M. (1981) 'Stress, coping and development', *Journal of Child Psychology and Psychiatry*, **26**(3).

Rutter, M. (1986) 'Child psychiatry: looking 30 years ahead', *Journal of Child Psychology and Psychiatry* **27**(6).

Rutter, M. (1991) 'Pathways from childhood to adult life: the role of schooling', *Pastoral Care in Education* **9**(3).

Sallis, J. (1996) 'A dangerous move', *Times Educational Supplement*, 16 February.

Salzberger-Wittenberg, I., Henry, G., Osborne, E. (eds) (1983) *The Emotional Experience of Learning and Teaching*. London: Routledge and Kegan Paul.

Saxe, G. B., Gearhart, M., Note, M. and Paduano, P. (1993) 'Peer interaction and the development of mathematical understanding', in Daniels, H. *Charting the Agenda*. London: Routledge.

Scharff, J. and Hill, J. (1976) *Between Two Worlds*. London: Careers Consultants.

Schein, E. H. (1969) *Process Consultation*. Harlow: Addison Wesley with Longman.

School Curriculum and Assessment Authority (1998) *Literacy and Numeracy in the Workplace*. London: SCAA.

Skynner, A. C. R. (1974) 'An experiment in group consultation with the staff of a comprehensive school', *Group Process* **6**.

Smith, V. P. (1996) 'Collaborative models of developing competence', *British Journal of In-service Education* **22**(3), 285–91.

Steel, J. (1998) *The role of the hospital school. Children UK 18*, 45. London: National Children's Bureau.

Steel, J. and Ofield, A. (1998) 'Empowering children in a hospital school', *Young Minds Magazine* **35**, 14–15.

Steinberg, D. (1989) *Interprofessional Consultation*. Oxford: Blackwell Scientific.

Steiner, G. (1998) 'Great music falls on deaf ears', *Guardian*, 22 August.

Stott, D. H. (1982) *Helping the maladjusted child*. Children with Special Needs Series. Milton Keynes: Open University Press.

Stow, L., Stringer, P., Hibbert, K. and Powell, J. (1992) *Understanding and Managing Difficult Behaviour: establishing staff support groups*. Newcastle upon Tyne: Educational Psychology Service.

Stringer, P. and Stow, L. (1992) 'Establishing staff consultation groups in schools', *Educational Psychology in Practice* **8**(2).

Taylor, D. (1994) 'Schools as a target for change: Intervening in the school system', in Dowling, E. and Osborne, E. (eds) *The Family and the School*. London: Routledge.

Teacher Training Agency (1998) *National Standards for Special Educational Needs Co-ordinators*. London: TTA.

Thornton, K. (1998) 'Primaries set to test 600,000', *Times Educational Supplement*, 4 September, 4.

Tizard, B. and Hughes, M. (1984) *Young Children Learning*. London: Fontana.

Turner, S., Robbins, H., Doran, C. (1996) 'Developing a model of consultancy practice', in *Educational Psychology in Practice* **12**(2).

Upton, G. and Cooper, P. (1991) 'Putting Pupils Needs First', *British Journal of Special Education* **18**(3), 111–13.

Vygotsky, L. (1978) *Mind in Society. The development of higher psychological processes*. Cambridge, Massachusetts: Harvard University Press.

Wagner, P. (1995) *School consultation: frameworks for the practising educational psychologist*. London: Kensington and Chelsea EPS.

Wall, W. D. (1973) 'The problem child in schools', *London Educational Review* **2**(2).

Warnock, M. (1996) 'Foreword' to Bennathan, M. and Boxall, M. *Effective Intervention in Primary Schools*. London: David Fulton Publishers.

Watkins, C. (1996) 'School Behaviour', *Viewpoint 5*, Newsletter, Institute of Education University of London.

Williams, E. (1998) 'Prison trauma', *Guardian Education*, 9 June, 4.

Williams, J. (1998) 'Let's not over-encourage', *Times Educational Supplement* **2**(1), 17.

Wilson, P. (1998) 'Select Committee Inquiry into "Berlin Wall"', (Report) *Young Minds Magazine* **34**, 3.

Winnicott, D. (1965) *The Maturational Processes and the Facilitating Environment*. London: Hogarth.

Winnicott, D. (1971) *Playing and Reality*. London: Tavistock.

Wolfendale, S. (1983) *Parental Participation in Children's Development and Education*. Reading: Gordon and Breach.

Wolff, S. (1969) *Children under Stress*. Allen Lane.

Woodhouse, D. and Pengelly, P. (1991) *Anxiety and the Dynamics of Collaboration*. Aberdeen: Aberdeen University Press.

Wragg, E. C. (1997) *The Cubic Curriculum*. London: Routledge.

Wrenn, A. (1998) 'Struck by love's dart', *Times Educational Supplement* **10**(4), 23–25.

Yapp, N. (1991) *My Problem Child*. Harmondsworth: Penguin.